The
Colourful World
of
CATS

The Colourful World of CATS

by
Stanley Dangerfield
Angela Sayer
Christine Metcalf
Mary Dunnill
Michael Findlay
Grace Pond
Olivia Manning
Gladys Hayward

Sundial

First published in 1975 by
Sundial Publications Limited
59 Grosvenor Street
London W1

Seventh impression, 1978

© 1975 Hennerwood
Publications Limited

ISBN 0 904230 09 0

Produced by
Mandarin Publishers Limited
Hong Kong

Contents

Introduction 6

The Care of
Kittens and Cats 8

Longhairs
and Shorthairs 22

The Family Cat 40

Siamese and
other Foreign Breeds 52

Feline First Aid 68

Cats On Show 84

Eastern Magic 94

Stars of
Television and Film 108

The Mind of the Cat 114

Index 127

Introduction

Stanley Dangerfield

Right
A pedigree Blue Burmese
at his most endearing.

Once upon a long time ago I interviewed John Freeman on television. At the time I must have been about the biggest dummy ever let loose inside a studio. John Freeman was the total professional, with a string of the most impressive 'face to face' interviews behind him that TV has ever seen.

This was a pet programme and the unaccustomed reversal of roles was accounted for by the fact that Mr Freeman owned two Abyssinian cats. And the fact that I was questioning the arch questioner explained why I was even more clumsy than usual. How else could I have blundered out with my first question? 'Why,' I demanded, 'do you dislike dogs?'

Of course Mr Freeman promptly explained that a love of cats did not necessarily presuppose a hatred of dogs. Mercifully I have forgotten the rest of the programme, except the moment when Pushkin (or was it Dulcie?) bit me. Twice. And hard.

People who associate me principally with dogs often ask me the same question – why I dislike cats. So let it be said that far from disliking them I have a private, as distinct from a public, passion for them. I admire them, respect them, love them. I recognize the many ways in which they are superior to dogs. And at the drop of a hat I will recount to the most hardened dog addict the reasons for such a view, even at the risk of being indicted for treason.

I cannot remember a time when I did not own a cat and I am certain that such a day will never come. A cat is an indispensable member of the family. True, I don't need a large number of cats around me to make the point. One is enough. And that is the size of the Dangerfield cat population, except when a stray temporarily graces the house with its presence.

Currently the cat is a Blue Burmese called – somewhat unimaginatively – Moggie. Of course he is beautiful. Beautiful, that is, if you are prepared to overlook somewhat donkey-like hind legs, a marked tendency to be overweight and a badly battered ear. Maybe the beauty is in his mind? Maybe. But strict regard for the truth forces the admission that, if present, it is well hidden. While he loves all humans, he seems to loathe all animals. Squirrels and baby bunnies which venture into the garden rarely survive to tell the tale. Big dogs pass the house on the other side of the road. Even horses appear to increase their speed as they trot past the front garden which is his stalking ground. And, sad to relate, my bird-loving neighbours once produced a petition requesting Moggie's removal, owing to his systematic and efficient raids on their bird tables. He was not after crumbs!

Yet even a hardened character such as Moggie is not all hostility. To see him with my pet dog is sheer joy. I keep Griffons, which are pint-sized busybodies born to torment and annoy any cat, especially their own. Moggie accepts their antics, suffers the indignities they heap upon him, tolerates even the pulling of his swishing tail. Then, with a pounce, he catches a young one, perhaps a quarter of his weight. Pins it to the ground with a powerful but deliberately harmless paw. And then washes it from head to foot. As I said, he's not all bad. How can he be when for the last twelve years I have never once had to give a pet Griffon a bath?

But that's more than enough about my cat in a book that is supposed to be about yours – about the cat or cats you already have, or the ones you are going to have. Which is as good a starting point as any.

The Care of Kittens and Cats

Stanley Dangerfield

*Left
A handsome, confident family cat glistening with health and enjoying an out-door life. Cats so full of character and fun are perfect companions for those who have not set their heart on a pedigree breed.*

*Below
The Manx is usually a strong character and an excellent companion.*

Although at the moment I keep a pure-bred cat, I am not wholly convinced that all pedigree cats are necessarily superior to all moggies, mousers or alley cats— call them what you will. Some pedigree cats are more pleasing to the eye than some cross-breds; but the reverse is also true. Some pedigree cats are better reared and therefore healthier than cross-breds; but once again this is not always the case.

It all adds up to the fact that I would not let breeding or the lack of it deter me from acquiring or keeping a cat that I liked. A good cat, like gold, is where you find it. Character is everything. And the chances are that character owes as much to environment as to heredity.

This admitted, many would still prefer a pure-bred, which means that they are faced with a bewildering choice. Deciding on a breed of dog is easy, because you have a good idea beforehand whether you want a giant or a pygmy, a killer or a softy, a tomboy companion for children or a cosy friend for a maiden aunt. A cat cannot be so conveniently classified.

Summary of the breeds

All cats are roughly the same size and have similar desires, appetites and characters. They do, however, have markedly different types of coat. So an early decision must be made—is it to be long or short? Bear in mind that although a Longhaired cat is frequently prettier it has the disadvantage of moulting more profusely and of requiring more grooming.

The list of the most popular Shorthaired breeds must be headed by the Siamese, Britain's top cat, brought here from Siam some 90 years ago. Most frequently their cream-coated bodies are tipped with seal-brown but the points can also be blue, chocolate, red, lilac, tabby or tortoiseshell. Perhaps the most dog-like of all cats, they love company, enjoy travelling in cars and will go for walks on the lead.

Burmese, either Brown or Blue, are similar to the Siamese in style and temperament but are possibly less vocal and slightly more respectful towards carpets, curtains and other soft furnishings.

Abyssinians are either rabbit-coloured or red and have distinctive ticking on each hair. They are particularly active and normally good-tempered and friendly, although some may be 'one man' cats.

The same can be said of the round-faced, comfortable-looking British Blues. But if you are seeking the unusual, consider the Manx cats. In any and every colour, these characters are unique in having unusually powerful hind legs, a loping gait and, as a rule, an entirely tailless, rounded rump.

Best known of the Longhaired varieties are the Whites, which can have either blue or orange eyes. Although spectacular at their best, regular grooming with powder is necessary to keep them that way.

Blue Persians certainly show the dirt less and have the same 'chocolate-box' appeal as well as a quiet, affectionate nature. They are used with Creams to produce Blue-Creams, looking too elegant to be true but still pure cats when it comes to sharing family life.

If you are looking for even more glamour, give some thought either to the Colourpoint, which has the colouring of the more exotic Siamese in addition to a long coat, or the Chinchilla, with its full, lush silver coat, brick-red nose and emerald-green eyes.

These are only a few of the more popular breeds on offer. I warned you the choice was bewildering!

The right kitten to buy
Being bewildered by the choice of breeds is nevertheless no excuse for losing your wits when faced by the practical proposition of buying a kitten. This needs to be approached with the minimum of sentiment and the maximum of cold, clinical deliberation. You could go to a pet shop and take pot luck. Or you could be smart and visit a couple of cat shows, which would enable you to meet breeders.

I feel quite strongly about seeing all young animals with their mother when making a purchase. It helps you to guess at the youngsters' adult appearance. It provides a guide as to the mother's health and the conditions under which the kittens have been reared. You can reassure yourself about their probable age.

Right
Even if you are an experienced cat breeder or a prospective cat owner with pre-conceived ideas, it is still easy to underestimate the appeal of a very young kitten such as this. If you are not ready to have a cat with you for years to come, you must resist the temptation.

Below
Kittens should be around eight weeks old when they are taken away from their mother, and preferably ten weeks old.

And, as a bonus, you might come away with the pick of the litter.

Before making a choice, watch the kittens at play. Then go for one that is sturdy, full of life, with wide-open, bright and sparkling eyes. Never choose a nervous kitten that runs and hides when you go to stroke it. Much better to pick out the individual that is playful and interested in everything that is going on. Kittens vary enormously in temperament and will be little changed in later life. So choose very carefully.

There are health signs which can easily be checked. The inside of the ears should be clean, without any smell or indications of discharge, which may be a form of canker. The nose should feel cool and slightly damp, not hot to the touch. Nose and eyes must also be quite free of discharge. The inside of the mouth should be rosy-pink, the tongue a normal red, and there should be a full set of tiny, clean white teeth.

The stomach should not appear swollen, which could indicate malnutrition or worms. No matter how long the fur, it should not cling, greasy and unkempt, close to the body; nor should there be any black 'coal-dust' specks in the coat, for these are spots of dirt left by fleas. The tail should be lifted up to make sure that there are no signs of diarrhoea.

A kitten should be between seven and ten weeks before you remove it from its mother. This gets the weaning period over but still allows time for socialization. An older cat which has spent too long in a cattery finds living with humans a rather trying business; and a stray rescued from a cat's home is likely to give even more trouble, perhaps being so set in its unfortunate ways that it never settles down comfortably in the household.

First days at home
When you first get your little blue-eyed innocent home, regard him as a suicidal escape artist. Keep the windows firmly closed and always keep a fire-guard in position. Electric fires are hazards and so too are all types of electric wire. Kittens have been electrocuted by playfully nibbling at wires leading to standard lamps and other electrical equipment.

The most important article to provide at this stage is a sanitary tray, filled with ashes, earth, saw-dust or a proprietary brand of litter. Kitten training must begin here. Cats, regardless of age, are inherently clean and prefer to relieve themselves outside when allowed to do so. If you have a garden this will solve hygienic problems but if not the tray will become a permanent fixture. In any event, have the tray available for the first day or two and make sure he is using it. Keep it where the kitten can easily find it, and change the contents whenever they have been soiled. In due course you can start escorting him to the garden at regular intervals, particularly after sleeping, eating and drinking.

A small cardboard box lined with a blanket is an ideal makeshift bed, which can later be replaced. A permanent bed can either be a basket, a type of canvas camp-bed or a wooden bench. Ideally it should be raised from the floor and be equipped with sides to keep out draughts. In my own home a 'dognest' bought for a puppy has proved a sensational success. This is a large loose cushion filled with polystyrene beads which gives way as the cat settles into it, providing both a cosy base and a firm surround.

Now all you have to worry about is feeding. But that will give you more than enough headaches for the first few weeks. It is not so much that a kitten has an enormous appetite, but that it has a small stomach and therefore needs frequent meals. No sooner have you finished one session than it seems you have to begin over again.

There are two stages in feeding kittens. The first is weaning, the second rearing. Since you will probably have bought your kitten fully weaned, the first will not normally apply. But it is just as well to know something about it, in case you later graduate, either by accident or design, to the role of breeder.

Weaning normally commences at around three weeks when the kittens should be encouraged to share their mother's food. A week or so later they should be lapping milk and eating some solid food. After another week they should be getting four meals a day; and at around seven weeks they ought to be fully weaned.

Protein-rich foods such as meat, fish and milk make the best diet, any type of meat or fish being acceptable. Alternatively, tinned proprietary food is suitable, providing the variety which prevents cats from becoming addicted to one type of food.

Since kittens grow fast and have relatively small stomachs, they require four meals a day when they are two to three months old, and three meals between the ages of three and five months. Milk should be given separately, and fresh drinking water must always be available.

Between six and eight months the period of rapid growth ends. At that point care must be taken, particularly with spayed cats, to avoid over-feeding which results in obesity.

When the natural caution and apprehension caused by the changed surroundings have worn off, the new kitten you have introduced to the household should soon settle. So, for that matter, should you! Then you will remember that your duty is to give him proper attention when he needs it, allow him to sleep when tired, feed him correctly and keep him warm. Nothing here, you will notice, about smothering him with sickly affection. For the moment, training is more important.

From kitten to cat
Keeping a cat in a flat presents an extra problem because there is not always a garden or facility for outdoor exercise. Consequently the cat must be allowed as much indoor freedom as possible; and if

Kittens enjoy each other's company the whole time. When you choose your kitten always consider whether you could not have two, particularly if your cats will be confined to a building. In a garden there is always plenty of insect and bird life to interest cats.

you have a balcony this can perhaps be wired in so that it can sleep in the sun. If there is no balcony, a light wire frame can easily be fixed to the window so that fresh air and sunlight can get in. These precautions are necessary because cats are often seriously injured as a result of falls from roofs or open windows.

If you have a garden, consider fitting a cat-flap, allowing the cat to go in and out at will. But remember that this will also enable him to bring his friends home once they learn how to open the flap!

Regardless of age, never shut a cat out at night. He may be involved in fights and return home injured; or he may get caught in the beam of headlights, being run over or causing an accident. His courting songs may not always be appreciated by neighbours. In inclement weather he risks exposure, perhaps leading to pneumonia. And there is even the chance he may get picked up by cat thieves.

Cats are the most independent of animals, deter-

mined only to do things when they are so inclined. Not for them the dog-like desire to please their owners. Although, if they feel like it, they can be trained to perform simple tricks, their cooperation cannot be relied upon. Nevertheless you should insist, right from the start, on certain patterns of behaviour.

Demand, therefore, that your pet does not clean or sharpen his claws on the furniture, curtains or carpet. A firm 'no' is soon understood. In the garden he can be encouraged to use a tree for this purpose. Failing this, buy a scratching post or log from a pet shop and fasten it fairly high up on a kitchen table leg. Once introduced to this, a kitten will quickly appreciate its purpose and use it regularly.

Set your mind firmly against such tricks as jumping onto the table and licking the butter dish or milk jug. Such behaviour may seem amusing when he is tiny, but the joke will soon wear thin. It is also unhygienic, and although you may be prepared to risk this, few

Below
Some cats are incurable thieves and even if you think your own cat would never steal, it is not wise to leave food lying around.

Right
The importance to cats of scratching is often underestimated. They like to flex their muscles and also get rid of old sheaths on the claws. Even if your cat has access to trees a scratching post will save your furniture. This is a Tabby Point Siamese.

of the friends you invite to tea will be as indulgent!

Don't be afraid to talk to your kitten—not such a foolish pastime as it sounds. Cats are great conversationalists and also, being polite, reply when spoken to. Two different sets of vocal chords enable them to produce a wide variety of sounds—some experts say more than one hundred—and very soon you will be able to identify those that demand the satisfaction of basic needs, including one that clearly means 'thank you'. Affection will be shown by a gentle touch of the paw, a lick of the tongue and by placing the paws around your neck. Purring, which seems to be quite involuntary, is a clear sign of contentment.

Provide plenty of playthings, such as rubber mice, pingpong balls or a small teddy bear. Some cats become very possessive over their toys, hiding them away and bringing them out only when they are in a playful mood. Most kittens like hide-and-seek, peering out from under chairs and around corners, scampering away with apparent glee.

By the time your kitten reaches the adult stage, there should be a quiet and satisfying relationship between you. You will have acquired an aesthetically pleasing addition to your household as well as a con-

Previous page
A Siamese kitten having
a good kick with his back
legs. Notice the top of
the sacking is already
torn to pieces where he
has scratched with his
front paws. Posts need
to be solid and heavy
to take the daily beating.

Two handsome and
self-confident tom cats.
There are many
convincing reasons for not
keeping non-pedigree
un-neutered male cats:
They are untidy about
the house and have a
tendency to go out and
fight with rival males.
This means that they
can be less affectionate
than other cats. Even
more important, they
produce unwanted
kittens which may be
uncared for and
ultimately stolen for
vivisection.

stant companion. Now for a serious word of advice. Unless you intend to go in for breeding, consider neutering. This will stop a male spraying around the house, leaving an unpleasant smell, and will also eliminate the tendency to wander off in search of females and to fight with rival males. Spaying a female kitten is equally important as it stops her 'calling' continually any time from the age of five to nine months onwards. Siamese are particularly noisy. During the mating period females constantly try to get out and neighbours' toms do their utmost to get in. The best person to advise is, of course, your vet, but it is a subject that everyone can sort out for themselves. My own view, however, is that the production of countless unwanted kittens is too serious a risk for any true animal lover to contemplate with complacency.

Grooming

Most cats seem to spend an inordinate length of time washing themselves. Even so, if dirt and dust, burrs, the odd flea, and any loose hair which might cause a furball are to be removed, you will still have to lend a hand. Although often ignored, grooming is a necessary part of daily care and you must certainly devote some time to it.

The tools required are a brush and comb. The brush should not be of wire but one with small, short bristles. The comb should be of the variety made especially for cats, with a wooden handle and metal teeth, the latter being set slightly closer for Short-haired cats. Another comb with very fine teeth will cure the flea problem, should this arise.

The best time to begin grooming is the day after the kitten arrives, because he will then learn from the start to appreciate it as an attention rather than resent it as a punishment. If you also play with him for a

while afterwards he will soon accept, even welcome, the entire routine.

During the grooming session, be sure to examine the ears. If they are dirty, wipe the inside of them with a piece of cotton wool. Should there be an objectionable smell or a discharge, do *not* run to the chemist to buy a canker lotion, which often does more harm than good. Ask the vet to take a look and prescribe the correct treatment for the particular ear infection involved.

A Shorthaired cat is simple to groom. Stand him on a newspaper-covered table, examine the fur for prickles and burrs, then comb thoroughly with the wide-toothed comb. If fleas are present or suspected, repeat with the fine-toothed flea comb. To do his stomach, sit with the cat lying on his back on your lap. Then give a final all-over polish by firm hand-stroking to promote sheen.

A Longhaired cat requires more attention and this,

of course, means more time. The long fur tends to tangle, particularly in spring and autumn, although daily grooming reduces this risk. Tangles must be gently teased out with the fingers or with a blunt knitting needle. Any that have been neglected may have to be cut away with round-tipped scissors although this should not have to be done. The coat will look a bit tatty at first but will recover in time.

A light-coloured cat can be sprinkled with talcum powder, followed by brushing and combing to remove stains. Bad grease stains can be eliminated with surgical spirit on a pad of cotton wool; and butter helps to remove tar from the paws. Tar and paint should never be tackled with chemical cleaners or solvents, some of which cause serious skin complaints.

Food for cats
Feeding, so far mentioned only as a form of 'first-aid' for the new kitten, requires further elaboration, be-

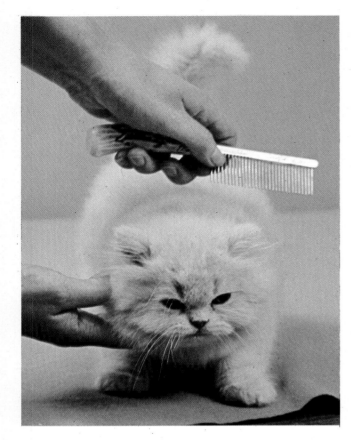

cause only if correct procedures are followed will your cat be able to enjoy a long and healthy life.

A wild cat, being carnivorous, lives by killing, gorging and then sleeping the banquet off for a day or two. A domestic cat could, in theory, do the same, and even the occasional day's starvation would not do much harm. But over the years it has become a nibbler and today it thrives best on two meals every day. Ideally the diet should consist of two-thirds animal flesh (including fish) and one-third cooked carbohydrate. A 10lb cat requires 3–4 oz twice a day.

Vitamins and minerals are also required and, fortunately, these are readily available. The important vitamins for a cat are A, which comes with liver, B1, in cereals and meat which is not over-cooked, and E, again found in liver. Despite its obvious value, however, liver should never form more than one-tenth of the total diet as it tends to promote loosening of the bowels, and in quantity may have a harmful effect, due to an excessive intake of vitamin A. Milk supplies both minerals and calcium and is, therefore, beneficial but can cause diarrhoea.

Tinned cat foods normally contain all the essential requirements of protein and carbohydrates as well as added vitamins and minerals. They are, therefore,

Left and Below
All cats enjoy being groomed regularly if they become accustomed to it when young. Longhaired cats in particular need to be groomed otherwise they may get fur balls from attempting to cope with matted fur themselves. Pedigree longhairs with a possible career in showing need extra attention. Cats particularly enjoy being brushed rather than combed, just as they do rolling in dust.

Right
Cats with silky long hair do seem to be less agile and adventurous than the shorthairs — the stance of this attractive marmalade cat is typical of a longhair — the body shape is clearly very different to that of the Orientals.

Previous page
Introduction of a Seal
Point Siamese stud to his
queen. This is an
excellent stud house with
a hot pipe running
through it and an
area outside for the stud
to exercise. It is wise
to go and visit the stud
and see the conditions in
which he lives before
sending your own queen
to him. The queen will
stay with her mate for
two or three days and
when she returns you will
have the stud's full
pedigree.

complete and balanced, convenient to store and simple to serve, as long as your cat will eat them.

Quantities are always difficult to recommend because appetites vary. The following is only a rough guide which should be adjusted if your cat becomes too lean or too fat. The animal's average daily requirement is approximately 200–250 calories, and this can be calculated roughly as follows: small tin of food = 200 calories; milk = 400 calories per pint; white fish and chicken = 500 per lb; liver and rabbit = 600 per lb; lean beef = 750 per lb; herring = 700 per lb. Now you can do your own sums!

Pedigree breeding

Having previously warned about the dangers of indiscriminate breeding, it may seem strange to end this chapter with some hints on how to breed. The difference, of course, is that this has to do with the planned breeding of pedigree cats. The emphasis on pedigree is not mere snobbery. The brutal truth is that far too many cross-bred kittens have brief and

miserable lives simply because they are valueless. The pedigree puss, however, being a very saleable commodity, is carefully looked after from the moment it is born to old age.

Pet males should, in my opinion, be neutered even if they do have pedigrees; but pedigree females can be kept for breeding provided you can put up with all the trouble. They come into season at around five to nine months and stay that way for between two and ten days. Some 'call' only two or three times a year, others every other week. Either way they will mate with any cat, which means constant watching unless you want a mongrel litter.

Prospective mothers should be at least ten months, if not a year old, and are normally sent to the stud for mating, preferably on the third day of 'calling'. The fee is payable in advance.

After returning home the queen, still being capable of mating, should be guarded. Mishaps aside, she carries her young for approximately 65 days, during which time she should lead a normal life. During the

Far left
A family of Eritish Blues
and a white stray kitten
which the mother is
fostering. This family
have a good strong
cardboard box lined with
newspaper which can be
changed frequently.

Left
A Seal Point Siamese
queen who escaped
during her calling period
and met a ginger tom.
The kittens are two days
old and will probably
grow into most
attractive cats with
Siamese and 'moggy'
characteristics.

last three weeks, however, she will want up to twice her normal food intake, so meals must be divided.

On the day she is due to give birth, regardless of any plans you may have made, most queens choose their own sleeping quarters. High on their list are wardrobes and, failing these, owners' beds. Sometimes this can be avoided by providing a wooden whelping box a week or so before the event. It should have easy access, be lined with newspapers, and placed in a dark cupboard.

The usual signs of imminent birth are restlessness and refusal of a meal. Soon after this labour will commence, indicated by a heaving of the flanks. Contractions usually follow with ever-diminishing frequency until a liquid discharge heralds the approach of the first kitten. This arrives in a sac, resembling a polythene bag, which the mother instinctively rips open with her teeth.

The mother then massages her kitten into active life by licking it with her rough tongue, after which she eases it towards her teats for suckling. The birth

of this first kitten is usually a slow process and may take up to an hour or more. Thereafter the kittens are normally delivered fairly quickly. The entire process may take from one to six hours, but unless the queen seems unreasonably distressed there is no cause for undue worry on your part. If problems do arise, call the vet promptly.

It is unwise to remove kittens from their box during the kittening process, and the whole family can be left for a few hours of recuperative sleep after it is all over. Then the queen can be given some warm milk, while the opportunity is taken to change the soiled bedding.

A feeding queen produces an enormous appetite and should be given up to three times as much food as she is normally. Quality is as important as quantity and the diet must provide vitamin A and calcium.

The kittens are born blind and open their eyes within a week or so. At three weeks they will be crawling and shortly after that weaning should commence.

Longhairs and Shorthairs

Angela Sayer

Left
A Longhaired Blue Persian with an excellent ruff and large full eyes with good colour.

Right
A Cream Longhaired kitten. Breeders have problems in breeding this variety true because of persistent tabby markings. These often show in the kittens but should disappear as they grow older. The eyes should be a beautiful brownish copper. This kitten still has the blue eyes of all kittens.

Pedigree cats can be divided into two basic types, defined by bone structure and overall conformation. The first group is close-coupled and stocky, round of head and eye, with small ears and short legs and tail. The second group is much lighter in build, long and lithe with slender bones, longer head, neck and tail and large pricked ears; most varieties in this latter group stand tall, their hind legs being longer than the forelegs. The first group, with which this chapter deals, is further categorized, according to coat length, into Longhaired (or Persian) cats and Shorthaired cats variously known as British Shorthaired, American Shorthaired, European Shorthaired and so on, depending on their country of origin.

The Persians

Longhaired cats, popular throughout the world, were first recorded in Europe at the end of the sixteenth century, when they were known as Angora cats, having been brought from Angora (now Ankara) in Turkey. Then, as further stock was imported from Persia (modern Iran) the name was changed to Persian Cat. It is from these original Angoras and Persians, as a result of careful and selective breeding, that the many beautiful Longhaired varieties of today have emerged.

These cats are known by different descriptive names to distinguish between the varieties, and slight variations in type are often apparent between them. All Persian cats, however, must have long, flowing silky coats and a full 'ruff' or frill around the neck which can be brushed up from the body to form a soft frame around the broad head. The standard of show points for perfection requires almost all Persians to have small, tufted ears, set well apart, and large, wide-awake eyes, plus a very short nose; but as will be seen the standard is somewhat modified in the breeds regarded as being only semi-Longhaired, for example, the Birman and the Turkish cats.

Most Longhaired cats are ideal for people who wish to own only one really decorative cat which is not too demanding or mischievous, yet which is affectionate and playful. All breeds may be kept quite successfully confined indoors if a toilet tray, a scratching post and some pot-grown grass for healthful nibbling are provided to compensate for lack of garden amenities. Persians are normally very healthy and hardy and need little special care except for grooming; but for this reason alone, folks with little spare time or patience should not take on any Longhaired breed, for the coats really do need constant attention with thorough brushing and combing every single day. The result of this daily titivation, combined with good feeding, will be a cat with bright eyes and a softly flowing coat. Careful handling from early kittenhood will help to ensure an even temperament and affectionate nature, and the daily grooming must be carried out gently and firmly so that it is never resented by the kitten.

The Self Longhairs

For convenience in showing, Persians are split into 'self' varieties—in which the cats are coloured uniformly—and 'other colours' which include the various tabbies, cats with the silver gene present, and cats with particoloured coats. The Self Longhaired group comprises Black, Blue, Cream, White and Red Persians.

Superior type in this group is shown by the most popular of all Longhaired breeds, the Blue Persian, which may have a coat of any shade of blue provided that the cat is quite uniformly coloured and that the colour is sound right down to the roots. Most fanciers of this variety prefer the paler coloured cats, and understandably so, for a pale blue, almost lavender toned Persian of exceptional type, prepared expertly for the show bench, is a sight of breathtaking beauty.

The Black Persian is also approaching perfection in type, and is most striking with its deep orange or copper eyes glowing from a coal-black face. Damp weather and a surfeit of sunlight can have an oxidizing effect on the coat of this variety, causing a rusty appearance which sometimes detracts from its full beauty. Kittens often have disappointingly shaded coats, although this effect clears as the new coat comes through. It is easy to understand why the raven-coated Black with its expressive face was once associated with witchcraft, demons and pagan rites.

The Cream, another variety in which type is outstandingly good, is nevertheless difficult to breed to perfection. The problems are encountered in trying to achieve coat colour sound to the roots, and uniform over the entire body. A pale cream shade is desired without any hint of tabby or bars. These blotched markings are very often seen in kittens which later grow into superior, clear-coated adults. White hairs, especially on the tail tip, are taboo. A good specimen of this breed with its burnished copper eyes can be a show-stopper, and a Cream Persian may often take the coveted Best in Show award in top class competitions.

White Persians may be Blue-eyed, Orange-eyed or even Odd-eyed, in which, as the name suggests, one eye is blue and one orange. Originally, all were of the Blue-eyed variety and many were found to be deaf, due to a malformation of parts of the inner ear, genetically linked with the eye colour. In attempts to breed out this distressing condition, outcrosses were made, to other Self varieties and the Orange-eyed White was produced, happily possessed of perfect hearing. Another result of this cross-mating was the appearance of the Odd-eyed White, which so delighted breeders, that this, too, was developed as a separate variety. In caring for the White Persian, daily grooming to ensure scrupulous cleanliness is even more vital, as soiled areas quickly become stained yellow and detract from the overall sparkling appearance.

The Red Persian is rare, and of less good type than the other Self varieties, possibly because judicious breeding to Blue and Black (which necessitates long-term planning in order to be successful) has been avoided in the past. It is very difficult to breed a cat free from tabby markings, and it is unfortunate that this most striking, copper-eyed variety so seldom graces the show bench today.

Tabby and silver genes

The Red Tabby Persian differs from the Self in having the classic marbled tabby pattern clearly etched in a deep, copper-toned red on a paler base coat, and eyes of deep orange. The white markings so often seen on non-pedigree counterpart of this variety are a very serious fault, and kittens showing any such markings are neutered and sold only as pets. Persian Tabbies may also be had in Brown or Silver, and the desired pattern is the same as for the Red. The Brown Tabby is perhaps the most natural-looking of all the Longhaired breeds, the classic pattern being densely defined in black on a rich tawny base, and the eye colour being hazel or copper. The Silver Tabby Persian is rare, but very beautiful with the black marbling on a clear silver ground, and green or hazel eye colour. One of the most difficult of the Longhairs to breed to perfection, type, in this, as well as the other Tabbies, is far less extreme than in the better Self varieties.

Another Persian achieved by the introduction of the silver gene responsible for the Silver Tabby, is one of the most exquisitely beautiful of all cats—the Chinchilla. In great demand as a model for films and advertising, this charming cat has a temperament well suited to such a glamorous career. Basically pure silver-white, each hair, on a good specimen, is tipped with black, producing an exotic, sparkling, ethereal look. The lustrous eyes, emerald or sea-green in colour, are outlined in black, giving them an unparalleled depth of expression. Although the cat is slightly lighter in build than other Persians, it is strong and firmly muscular without ever appearing

A Black Persian

Left
The Longhaired Orange-eyed White. This cat is of excellent type with widely spaced ears well set on the head. The Blue-eyed Longhaired White far right, is the original and much older breed, but as blue-eyed cats are very often deaf, breeders introduced crosses with other self coloured breeds and produced the spectacular Orange-eyed cat.

Above
A beautiful Red Persian. This is a rare breed and they are very difficult to produce to standard. Many of the kittens retain their tabby markings or are rather pale in colour like the 'moggy' ginger and marmalade cats.

Right
The Brown Longhaired tabby is perhaps the most natural looking of all the more highly bred cats. The eyes should be hazel or copper in colour and the classic markings clearly defined in black.

Page 29
A champion Chinchilla and her four-week-old kitten. Chinchillas are slightly smaller than other Persians although they are strong and healthy cats and have very gentle and affectionate natures.

coarse, and overall type is extremely good. Very heavily ticked Chinchillas are recognized as a separate breed in some countries, and known as the Shaded Silver Persian.

The unique colouring of the Smoke Persian, with a body of jet black shading down to pure silver at the roots and on the sides and flanks, is also due to the presence of the unusual silver gene. The mask and feet are densely black, while the frill and ear tufts are silver. With the usual massive Longhaired build and enormous orange or copper eyes, the Smoke is a very impressive creature. The Blue Smoke cat is also recognized in many countries but is not quite so striking in appearance, as the dilute blue colour replaces the black of the normal Smoke, and also tends to diffuse into the base colour.

Females to the fore

Tortoiseshell, Tortoiseshell-and-White and Blue-Cream Persians are almost without exception female only. This is because the Red colour (or yellow, as it is known by geneticists) is due to a semi-sex-linked genetic factor. The tortoiseshell is the female counterpart of the Red Self male, an appealingly patchworked creature of red, cream and black in well-defined areas

Left
A Blue-Cream Longhaired cat with excellent inter-mingled pastel shading. These Persian cats are invariably female and are the result of cross breeding between Blues and Creams. Breeders have worked out a breeding pattern so that the colours of the kittens are predictable. They are striking cats with deep orange eyes glowing against the misty effect of the coat.

Below
Another variety which is only female is the Tortoiseshell-and-White. These are dilute Tortie and White Persians when the black becomes blue and the red is paler. The white patches should be clear but not predominant.

over the head, legs, body and tail. The most attractive specimens also have a prominent red or cream blaze running down the mask between the deep orange or copper eyes. The Tortie-and-White is very similar, except that white patches must be present though not predominant in addition to the red, cream and black. As there are no fertile Tortoiseshell males, the lovely females are best bred to self-coloured cats, and give birth to fascinating mixed litters. If a Black stud is used, the resulting litter may have either Black or Red male kittens, or some of each, while the females will be Black or Tortoiseshell like the mother. If a Red Self male is used, the male offspring can again be Red or Black and there could be some Red females in addition to Black and Tortoiseshell kittens of the same sex.

Tortie-and-White females are usually mated to Bicoloured males to help control the amount of white produced in the kittens; and the colour of the kittens will depend upon the choice of male in the same way as in the case of the Tortoiseshell, except that each will have the desired white markings in addition to the three basic Tortoiseshell colours.

The Blue-Cream Persian is among the top few breeds for excellence of type and is the female counterpart of the Cream variety. Blue-Cream females mated to Cream males produce both Blue and Cream male kittens and Blue, Cream or Blue-Cream female kittens in the same litter. Mated to a Blue male, the same offspring may be expected, with the exception of the Cream females. One of the most aesthetically appealing of all Persians, the softly intermingled pastel blue and pinkish-cream of the coat gives a misty, flowing look, and the contrast provided by the deep copper or orange eyes is quite startling.

The Bicoloured Longhair is, as the name implies, a cat of two colours—either Red-and-White, Black-and-White, Blue-and-White or Cream-and-White. The colours must be present in equal amounts and for perfection the chin, neck, shoulders, forelegs and feet should be pure white. In addition, a neat white blaze should bisect the face. The most common of the Bicolours is the Black-and-White variety, often affectionately referred to as the 'Magpie'. The eye colour in this variety is required to be either copper or deep orange, and green or yellow eyes are considered to be show faults. The coat must have clearly coloured areas on the white, and these must not contain any white hairs, spots or patches.

The eastern influence
In recent years, the Himalayan factor has been introduced into the Persian breed. This is the genetic factor responsible for the exotic colouring of Siamese cats. It ensures that the cat's coat colour is restricted to the extremities of the body, namely the mask, ears, tail and paws, and that blue eye colour is also produced. A few very dedicated breeders, using selective breeding methods and carefully planned family trees,

Above left
A Turkish or Van kitten with excellent bright orange markings. These cats have very soft silky coats which are a dense chalky-white in colour.

Left
A Bi-coloured Longhair cat well marked with even patches of cream and white.

Above
A Blue Smoke Persian. These cats can be very striking indeed, particularly the Black Smoke when the contrast between the coat colours is greater. The under coat is silver, shading to the over coat of jet black or blue at the tip. The mask and feet are of solid black or blue while the ruff and ear tufts are of silver.

priest had a white cat as his oracle, and together they sat before the golden statue of the sapphire-eyed goddess Tsun-Kyan-Kse in the temple of Lao-Tsun, sharing their meditations. Raiders killed the priest one day, and the faithful cat Sinh laid its head against the silver hair of its murdered master, all four paws placed upon the body. A miracle occurred—the white fur turned as golden as the light radiating from the goddess, the yellow eyes took on her sapphire hue, while the ears, nose, legs and tail became as brown as the earth. Only the paws, still in contact with the dead priest, remained white, denoting his purity. Refusing all nourishment, Sinh remained to guard the body for seven days, then died, taking the perfect soul of its master into heaven. From that day the appearance of all the temple cats changed in the same miraculous manner. Since that day, whenever a sacred temple cat dies, it is said that the soul of a priest ascends with it to heaven.

Recent additions

A semi-Longhaired cat, really deserving a category of its own, is the Turkish or Van Cat. This gained a reputation for being very fond of swimming when first brought out of Turkey by an intrepid English lady in 1955. It is not really true, however, to say that this breed seeks out water in order to swim. Like most cats, it is a good swimmer, but is rather less averse than other breeds to water. The Turkish cat does not have the extreme type of the more usual Persians. Its chalk-white coat is of medium length, the silky hair patched with deep, bright auburn markings on the head, plus a bushy auburn tail. With large, round amber eyes and delicately pink nose leather and pads, it is most unusual in appearance and quite delightful to own.

have now produced a whole range of fascinating 'pointed' Persians, known in some countries as Colourpoint Persians and in others as the Himalayan. These cats are not simply Longhaired Siamese but true Persian cats in type, conformation and coat length. The distinctive colouring is, however, restricted to the points alone, and the eyes are always blue. So far they exist as Seal, Blue, Chocolate, Lilac, Red and Tortie Points, and it is quite feasible that any and all 'Siamese' colours will eventually appear—Cream, Chocolate-Cream, Blue-Cream, Lilac-Cream, and Tabby in Seal, Blue, Chocolate and Lilac. What has proved so hard to achieve in this variety is the deep blue eye colour. Many examples have pale, watery-blue eyes, causing breeders to intensify their efforts to increase the density of the blue colouration so that it approaches that of the standard Siamese.

The Birman or Sacred Cat of Burma may at first glance look very like the Colourpoint. But although the same genetic Himalayan factor is responsible for the restriction of the colouring to the points, this ancient breed does differ considerably in appearance. The Birman is bred only in Seal-pointed or Blue-pointed forms, and the body is longer than that of other Persian cats, as is the length of nose and tail. The most distinctive feature of the Birman however, is the presence of flawless white 'gloves' on all four paws, extending on each hind leg to a point, rather like a gauntlet.

Legend has it that hundreds of years ago, a Kittah

During the initial matings necessary for producing the Colourpoint Persians, the chocolate gene, only previously found as a dilution of Seal Point in Siamese cats, was introduced into some Longhaired lines and caused two very rare and beautiful new Self-coloured varieties to emerge. Where the chocolate gene was present in both sire and dam, Longhaired kittens were born of a uniform milk-chocolate shade all over, and when both parents carried the blue factor in addition to the chocolate, some delicately pale lilac kittens also appeared in those litters. Having lustrous orange eyes, the two new varieties were thought to be most attractive by several fanciers, and breeding programmes were drawn up to develop them into well-typed Persian varieties.

Many more new varieties are genetically possible in the Persian ranks and some, owing their origins to the elusive silver gene, are occasionally seen at the larger cat shows at various stages of development. Included in these 'Any Other Colour' classes are such cats as the Blue Chinchilla and the Cameo. Both are very similar to the Chinchilla, with changes in basic coat colour and ticking. The Blue Chinchilla looks extremely exotic, being heavily ticked with steel blue against a pale blue base. The Cameo Persian Cats have the red gene present, and three varieties are presently being developed, each of which can also be dilute (cream rather than red), giving six alternative shades. The palest of the group is the Shell Cameo, which has a pure white undercoat and palest apricot-pink ticking. The Shaded Cameo is considerably darker than the Shell, with quite intense red or cream shading gradually to white on chin, chest and belly. Even deeper toned is the Smoke Cameo with its white undercoat shading to a deep red-beige, and with deep red points and mask enhanced by the white ruff and ear tips. The Shell and Shaded Cameos have beautiful rose-pink eye-liner and nose leather, and their eye colour may be deep orange or copper, while those of the Smoke Cameo may be either copper or gold. The many problems besetting the pioneer breeders of these unusual cats have been largely surmounted, and a fine nucleus of unrelated breeding stock has been established, ensuring that the Cameo Persian is here to stay.

The Shorthairs

Many of the British shorthaired varieties are merely short-coated versions of their Persian cousins and all conform to a basic standard of points of perfection. British cats must have a sturdy body, medium in length and with a broad chest. The legs are shortish and the paws, round and neat, while the tail is short and fairly thick. The large round head is topped with small ears, having plenty of width between, the eyes

are full and round, and the nose short. The short close coat must never feel harsh or be open, but feel firm to the touch, with a pleasant texture. It is easy to keep in immaculate condition, only requiring once-weekly brushing and combing, although a thorough hand-grooming should be carried out each day as this keeps the muscles toned up, removes all dead hair and imparts a healthy sheen to the animal.

To the layman, some British Shorthaired breeds may seem to be no more than particularly striking examples of ordinary house pets; but the pedigree Shorthairs are of sound background and have inbred health, stamina and excellent temperaments (making them ideal for showing). As pets, they are intelligent, charming and extremely affectionate. Less mischievous than their Oriental cousins, the British Short-haired breeds are graceful and active, fond of outdoor exercise, and are best kept in homes where they may have the run of the garden.

It is believed that the forebears of the British Short-hair came by ship from both the east and the north. The Phoenicians and the Romans probably introduced tabby-type cats, whereas the cats brought in by the Vikings evidently had thicker, double coats. Long before the Viking era, in fact, blue shorthaired cats are reported to have been kept in Scandinavia. It was from these early arrivals that the lovely and varied breeds of British Shorthair have gradually been developed over the centuries.

Aristocrats of the show bench

Most popular of all the British cats is the Blue, often described as the aristocrat of the Shorthairs. The well-knit powerful body is covered by a lovely thick, close-lying coat of light to medium blue, which is admirably set off by large, lustrous copper or orange eyes. The coat must be sound without any tabby markings or bars and no odd white hairs. Originally, this breed was a dark slate-blue, and much injudicious cross-breeding was carried out with Russian and Siamese cats, and also with Blue Persians. Recently, however, the breed has been more carefully nurtured and the general standard at shows is very high.

Although the world is full of handsome Black Shorthaired cats it seems, it is no easy task to breed and rear a near perfect pedigree specimen to its exacting standard of points, and the most difficult problem to be overcome is the elimination of white hairs. The kittens are often brownish-black, and this effect is also often seen in adults who have been exposed to very damp conditions, or too much sunlight. The eye colour required in this variety is copper or deepest orange, any trace of green in the eye being a serious fault. A really good British Black can be buffed-up with a chamois leather until it gleams like polished ebony, and with its glowing eyes defies anyone to doubt its ancestry.

British Whites, like White Persians, come in three types—Orange-eyed, Blue-eyed and Odd-eyed. The

Left
Seal and Blue Point Birman kittens. Notice the attractive white gauntlets on the back legs.

Right
A Shaded Cameo cat. The Cameo Persians are similar to the Chinchillas in that each hair is tipped with a darker colour than that of the under coat. The Shaded Cameo has quite intense red or cream shading, with deep orange eyes. Cameos were bred originally from Chinchillas but with the introduction of the red factor. Breeders are now using a Blue-Cream female and a Smoke male to avoid the Chinchilla's green eyes.

Left
A Shorthaired Red Tabby with a rich russet-coloured coat.

Below
A Shorthaired Cream kitten with faint tabby markings on the face and body. These will go as the kitten grows older.

same problems with deafness have been encountered in the Blue-eyed variety. It is thought that a Blue-eyed White Shorthair born with black smudges on the crown of the head will have perfect hearing, although the smudges fade and completely disappear as the kitten grows. The White varieties are all very sweet and docile and make delightful affectionate pets. They need little grooming, just a weekly brush and comb through to remove dead hairs, but the tail ends must be watched, for if soiled and neglected, an unpleasant yellow staining appears which is difficult to remove.

One of the oldest established British breeds is the Cream, yet it is quite rare, even at the largest cat shows, possibly because the standard, which calls for a rich cream colour, with no bars or tabby marks, is very exacting and difficult to reproduce. A good specimen,

with its copper or hazel eye colour and typical massive build is a most arresting sight; but despite the efforts of a small band of dedicated breeders, really good kittens are in very short supply the world over.

The female equivalent of the Cream is the Blue-Cream, a very useful cat to have as a breeding queen, for, depending upon her chosen mate, she may have Blue, Cream, and Blue-Cream kittens. This cat is most attractive, the palest blue and pinkish-cream hairs softly intermingling to give an almost shot-silk look, especially in a good clear light. The soft, fine-textured coat is easy to keep in immaculate condition with the minimum of grooming, but the loose dead hair should be combed out weekly to prevent them being swallowed by the cat and producing a hairball. The Blue-Cream, whose eyes may be copper, orange or yellow,

Far left
The British Blue is one of the most popular of the Shorthaired cats and they breed very well to type.

Below
An Odd-eyed White.

makes a charming house pet, tending to devote its affection to a particular member of the family, and is very intelligent, often scooping up its food with a dainty paw and preferring to drink from a dripping tap rather than from a water bowl.

Tabbies

Blotched, striped and spotted cats have been depicted in scrolls and ancient records, and the majority of mongrel and wild cats are marked with some form of tabby pattern. Selective breeding has ensured, however, that pedigree Tabbies are quite distinct from their cousins of unknown ancestry. Three colours are recognized in the British tabby pattern, and a very exact and classic marbled pattern is essential in show and breeding stock, whatever the coat colour. The classic tabby pattern has marks resembling a butterfly on the shoulders and swirls of oyster patterns on the flanks. A large letter 'M' marks the forehead, and the neck has two necklaces or mayoral chains encircling

it. Rings on legs and tail must be evenly distributed and clearly defined, and there must be no trace of white hairs in any of the three varieties, a white tip to the tail being a particular fault.

Perhaps the best of the Tabbies, for type, is the Silver, a truly exquisite creature with jet-black markings showing clearly against the pure silver ground colour and offset by clear, distinctly green eyes. Showy, yet shy and gentle, the Silver Tabby Shorthair has recently become very popular throughout the world, and classes at most shows are well filled with worthy examples of the variety.

The Brown Tabby, with its pansy-like expression, is, perhaps the most 'ordinary' of the pedigree breeds, for the really russet-brown coat colour of pre-war days is hard to achieve and rarely seen today. The standard calls for dense black markings in the classic pattern on a rich sable or brown base, and the eye colour may be either orange, hazel, deep yellow or green. The worst fault seen in this breed is a white

Above
A Tortoiseshell-and-White Shorthair.

chin, the ideal being cream or light brown. Only careful selection of breeding stock can eradicate this shortcoming.

A Red Tabby cat of good type and colour is rare, but well worth seeking out if one requires a sure-fire show winner. While its mongrel counterparts are sandy or marmalade, the pedigree Red Tabby has a coat with the ground colour of a deep even orange-red, with densely etched classic markings in a much darker tone. The eyes are deep orange or hazel.

The widely held belief that all Red cats are male and that any female that does turn up is worth a small fortune is, unfortunately, not true. Red male cats can be produced from Tortoiseshell or Red mothers, mated to any coloured stud male, but only if the Tortoiseshell or Red mother is mated to a Red male will a Red female kitten be born, due to the sex-linkage of the genetic factor involved. Red Tabby females mated to Red Tabby males will, however, give birth only to Red Tabby kittens, of both sexes.

Coats of many colours
The Tortoiseshell Shorthair is among the oldest known of all varieties, being depicted in paintings centuries old. The fine, glossy coat of this all-female variety makes it easy to prepare for showing with the minimum of grooming, and its delightful nature makes it a perfect house pet. The variety must be evenly patched in black, red and cream and must not have any white hairs, or tabby or brindled markings. It is important that the legs, face and tail are as evenly patched as the body, and a red blaze, bisecting the face, is desirable. The large, expressive eyes may be orange, copper or hazel.

Once known as the Spanish cat, and called the Calico Cat in the United States, the Tortoiseshell-and-White Shorthair is another all-female variety which is difficult to breed to standard, most kittens having too much white and lacking coloured patches on their legs. Recently, Black-and-White and Red-and-White Bicolour males have been used in breeding, with greatly improved results. The few males of the variety which are born from time to time all proved to be sterile.

Bicolour cats were originally expected to be marked as precisely as Dutch rabbits, but it was soon apparent that this standard was too exacting, with an excessive number of good cats having to be discarded for breeding purposes because they did not quite conform. The standard was then amended and now demands that

Below
A Silver Spotted kitten and a Silver Tabby. Tabby and Spotted kittens can appear in the same litter and it is important that the markings of the Spotted cat do not merge into one another. They should contrast well with the background.

the patching is clear and evenly distributed, with not more than two-thirds of the coat being coloured and not more than half of the coat being white. Bicolours may be bred in any colour plus white, and a white blaze down the mask is highly desirable. The white areas must be free from coloured patches and the coloured areas free from white hairs, exactly as in the equivalent Persian variety. The eyes should be deep copper or orange.

Spots and stumps
Although spotted cats have been recorded throughout history, even in the Dead Sea Scrolls, it was not until 1966 that they were officially given recognition in Great Britain as a *bona-fide* breed. Type is as for all the British Shorthairs, with a powerful, well-knit body, shortish, thick tail, broad, full-cheeked head and a short, fine and close-lying coat. The spots may be either round, star-shaped or triangular, and the spotted pattern carries more points in judging than type.

Spotted cats may be Silver, Brown, Blue, Red, Cream, or any other definite colour and the eye colour must correspond to the standard required by their Tabby equivalents. The Silver Spotted, looking like a

miniature snow leopard is not only the most spectacular of all the British spotted varieties but arguably the most exotic of all British Shorthaired breeds.

Last, but by no means least of the recognized British breeds, is the mysterious Manx, the tailless cat first found on the Isle of Man and purported to have been washed ashore from a Spanish ship wrecked there in 1588. Manx cats are not prolific breeders, due to the factor which makes them tailless and which also sometimes adversely affects the unborn kittens, causing them to be resorbed by the mother, and thus be stillborn.

These cats are most amusing pets to own and develop their own unique characters in human company. They may be of any recognized cat colour or pattern with the matching eye colour and can be either Rumpy – the completely tailless type – or Stumpy, with a tiny tail. Sometimes, even when two Rumpy Manx are mated together, the kittens born have normal tails! Having much longer legs at the hind end gives the Manx cat a characteristic, rabbit-like gait. Furthermore, because the unique, double coat is soft and open like that of a rabbit, it is not surprising that the breed was once thought to be the result of a cross between a cat and a rabbit.

Left
A red and white Manx cat with her tabby kitten. Notice this kitten does in fact have a tail although it is still a Manx. The father of this kitten was also a tail-less cat so the kitten is a throw-back.

Right
The Chinchilla is still many people's favourite cat and is picked most often to pose for photographs or films.

The Family Cat

Christine Metcalf

Two healthy active family cats in beautiful condition. Cats love to roll in grass and also eat it – it is a good emetic. The coat of a shorthaired black is one of the most striking when it is in top condition. Notice also how bright his eyes are.

The cat is no newcomer to the family hearth. It took up residence centuries ago when man was still a cave-dweller. According to the stories, it was initially attracted by the warmth of the fire—a suggestion that is not difficult to accept as one watches the cat on a chilly evening in a relaxed heap before the fireside or on a summer day basking in a sunny spot in the garden.

The cat is fond of its creature comforts and, where these are provided to its taste, will strike a fair bargain by giving in return loyalty and companionship. However, the cat is both shrewd and discerning, and will rarely stay in a place if it decides otherwise. The fact

that you have to earn its affection lends support to the commonly voiced opinion that, far from choosing a cat, it chooses you.

This should not present any problem so long as you observe the code for mutual happiness. Basically, this entails proper care for its physical needs, such as regular feeding, grooming and cleanliness; but there are other considerations to take into account when accepting a cat into your life.

Before acquiring a kitten, it is worth taking a careful look at the characteristics of the different breeds. Apart from the obvious fact that no two cats are alike,

every one having a unique personality, each breed possesses individual features; and if you are attracted to one more than another, it is advisable to consult a reputable breeder. On the other hand, you may have no choice in the matter, simply being asked to give house room to a friend's unwanted kitten. Nevertheless, be it aristocrat or moggy, a cat has basic needs which demand to be satisfied.

The kitten's homecoming

Moving your new kitten from a familiar setting to a strange environment can be very alarming for the small creature. Being cooped up in a basket and taken for a car journey will be brand new experiences. Its mother is no longer there to teach and comfort it, and the brothers and sisters who have been constant playmates are also suddenly missing. When the time comes to sleep there are no other furry creatures of its own kind to form a bundle of warmth. Abruptly it is faced by complete strangers in new surroundings—a dis-

Above Left
Two kittens greet each other and find out where the other has been. Kittens and cats often do this before dashing off to play together.

Left
Cats and dogs can become great friends if care is taken over the initial introductions. These can take some time and you will need patience if you are bringing a young animal into a family where there is already a well established dog or cat.

Above
The outside world provides an exciting hunting ground for cats as it contains so many small creatures. This cat is stalking and will pounce on his prey after much wriggling and swaying from side to side. Often enough the prey is in the cat's imagination or is merely a leaf or twig which is fun to play with.

turbing situation at the very least. So the transition from pet shop or cattery to a new home must be handled with the greatest care.

The best time to introduce your kitten is when most members of the family are likely to be around, as during the school holidays. But it must be done by gradual stages. When you first arrive home, take the kitten to a place where it can rest without being disturbed by children or by other animals. A good sleep will help to calm it whereas a boisterous family reception will only frighten it all the more. When it wakes up and has had some refreshment, allow it to explore the house but do not let it out of your sight in case it runs into danger or loses its way.

The shock of coming into a new home can be lessened by providing a close and already familiar companion in the shape of another kitten from the same litter. The little extra expense and effort involved are well rewarded by the friendship you and they will share. Two cats brought up together are never far apart. They can work off all their excess energy by playing with each other, there will be no chance of loneliness during the day if everyone is out of the house, and they can be placed in the same cattery together when the family are on holiday.

Kittens and children
On no account acquire a kitten for your children unless you are willing to take responsibility for looking after it. Youngsters can rarely sustain their interest all the time, becoming so absorbed in other activities such as games, hobbies and homework, that a kitten's mealtime can easily be overlooked. What is more, never give a kitten or any other domestic animal as a gift to a child before first obtaining the consent of the parents. Children often tire of a pet when it loses its baby appeal, and if the adults are not particularly interested either, the pet becomes unwanted. It is sad

when this neglect occurs, as it is not easy to find a new home for a grown animal.

Children tend to love a kitten rather fiercely and must be warned to handle it gently. A tiny bundle of soft fur is very cuddly but the bones are extremely fragile. Avert disaster by teaching them the correct way to hold a kitten, with one hand under the chest while the other goes around and under the back, supporting the weight on the arm. Never allow a kitten to be picked up by the back of the neck as this may cause muscle damage.

A cat loves to play, not only for pure pleasure but also for the exercise. Here too, however, some instructions on do's and don'ts are essential. Simple toys are best. Chasing and retrieving a piece of paper rolled into a ball and thrown across the floor is a favourite game; and a length of string dangled from a height or trailed along the ground is good practice for the hunting instincts. Tying the string to an empty cotton reel will prevent the end from being swallowed.

Pictures in books and papers sometimes show animals wearing clothes—all very charming as entertainment, but liable to put the wrong ideas into the heads of small children. Trying to squeeze a kitten into a doll's dress is a practice to be severely discouraged because the animal's little joints may easily be dislocated.

Like every baby, a kitten tires rapidly and must be allowed to sleep frequently. Its rest should be undisturbed, and it is often necessary to remind children that the time has come to stop playing for a while.

Kittens and other pets
Introducing a kitten into a household where there is already an established pet creates a situation that requires tactful handling but which is basically a matter of applying common sense and diplomacy. An adult cat will not accept a newcomer as readily as will

a dog or other animal. The explanation for this is simply territorial ownership. In the wild state a cat has to protect its boundaries in order to safeguard its food supplies. Our domestic pet has inherited this basic instinct from its ancestors, and a newly introduced kitten will possess the same intuitive traits. If challenged, its reaction will be to turn into a ball of spitting, hissing fury. The older inhabitant, accustomed to dispatching all garden intruders in no uncertain fashion, is suddenly faced by a miniscule stranger with the temerity to ruffle its fur and behave aggressively. No wonder it asserts its superiority by cuffing the impertinent little creature's ears. This type of angry confrontation may be amusing for the onlookers but can be distressing and even painful for the participants.

Given prudent handling, such a situation can be avoided and a good relationship allowed to develop naturally. So when you bring the kitten into the home, keep it apart from other established pets in a separate room and make the introduction gradually. All parties must be allowed to adjust to the idea and to settle down to unfamiliar smells before being left together unsupervised. Many unlikely friendships have been forged between cats and other animals (including birds and mice), but you must be around all the time during the early stages to prevent disaster.

In the course of the kitten's many sleeping periods

Above right
A cat door is invaluable. It is easy to fit and once you have taught the cat how to get in and out there is no longer any tie upon you or frustrations for the animal. A flap that is fairly stiff to swing will deter other interested neighbouring cats.

Right
Silver Tabby and Silver Spotted kittens playing around a large kitten pen. A pen is very useful when the kittens are old enough to be away from their mother but too young to be left without surveillance. You can put them out in the sun or confine them indoors.

Far right
A Lilac Point Siamese with powerful paws using a bird table as a scratching post. The kitten will very quickly learn to do the same.

you should take the opportunity to fuss and pet the other animals, for this will help them to become reconciled more easily to the presence of an additional member of the household. Animals, like children, crave constant affection and will show jealousy if not reassured.

The self-sufficient cat

Rudyard Kipling wrote of the cat: 'He walked by himself and all places were alike to him.' Folk who do not really know and understand the cat might assume that the writer was describing a single-minded and selfish creature; but those of us who are devoted to the animal know that this very independence is an admirable quality, stemming from the fact that, like its wild relatives, it is a solitary hunter. So when it is out and about it is always alone. This does not mean that it shuns company – on the contrary – but it is selective in choosing friends. The dog will go hunting in packs and leap about the neighbourhood looking for others of its kind to join in play; but the cat enjoys only the company of other cats it knows well – members of the same household.

One great advantage of living with a cat is that it does not need to be exercised, for play is itself the best form of exercise. A garden, affording the freedom to come and go at will, is a great boon but by no means indispensable. If you do have a garden it is a simple matter to fix a cat-flap to one of the outside doors of the house, which will give your pet complete liberty. The opening need not be large (about 6 × 4 inches) but it should swing vertically so that it can be opened from either side. If the flap is fitted with weights it will swing slowly, thus preventing the tail from being trapped. But the opening must be kept well away from bolts and locks so as to deny easy access to burglars.

Daily grooming is necessary to remove loose hair or any odd flea that may have been picked up. In other respects the cat is instinctively a very clean animal, easily house-trained. A garden naturally solves hygienic problems, but for the flat-dweller a litter tray must be provided.

A cat needs to scratch in order to keep claws in trim. The act of scratching removes the outer shell as it becomes worn, leaving new, beautifully sharp claws ready for hunting and climbing. It also enables the muscles and tendons to be kept in good condition. For this reason – and in order to prevent your carpets and furniture from being damaged – a scratching post is an important piece of equipment. Such a post can be bought or made by covering a solid board with a piece of carpet. By holding the kitten's paws and going through the motions of scratching on the post, you can teach it to leave the furniture alone. In this, as in toilet training, there may be the occasional mishap or moment of forgetfulness, in which case just be firm and show it once more what you expect of it. Never become angry, for this will only confuse and

45

frighten the kitten; and on no account strike it, because this may easily cause an injury.

Holiday time

Pets often present a problem for their owners at holiday time and this is sometimes given as an excuse for not keeping them in the first place. It is during the holiday season that animal sanctuaries are faced with a larger than usual number of strays, simply because owners have omitted to make adequate arrangements. Fitting an easy access route such as a cat-flap, putting down a large supply of food and then leaving a cat alone to ration itself to a daily allowance is quite unacceptable. The cat would almost certainly indulge in an orgy of gluttony, leaving none for later. Even catering for its greed by supplying too much food must inevitably result in left-overs that would turn stale or be contaminated by flies. In either case the health and wellbeing of the cat would be bound to suffer.

A useful solution is to arrange with a reliable neighbour to provide regular meals, but it is important to find someone really dependable. Although the cat will miss you, it will remain in familiar surroundings and the upheaval will not be so great. An alternative arrangement is to take your pet to a recognized cattery. There are a number of boarding establishments of this type, some good, others bad. Where possible, personal recommendation is preferable. Advertise-ments are usually to be found in local papers, and your vet, being familiar with the neighbourhood, should be able to advise.

A visit to the cattery before making a booking is, in any event, well worthwhile. The most important thing to look for is cleanliness, for unless the place is scrupulously hygienic your pet will be at risk. Look particularly at the litter trays, make sure that the house is warm, dry and light, and confirm that there is sufficient space in the pen for exercise as well as a scratching post.

Good accommodation gets fully booked early in the holiday season, so plan well ahead. You will probably be asked to supply a certificate to the effect that your cat is in good health and that it has been inoculated against feline infectious enteritis, so arrange for that as well.

When placing your pet in a cattery it is a good idea to take along its sleeping blanket or a favourite soft toy, for the smell of something familiar will provide a bit of security.

A cattery is especially valuable if you are taking a holiday abroad. Quarantine regulations require that any cat entering this country should spend six months isolated in a quarantine cattery. The fact that an animal may only have been abroad for a short time on a vacation will not affect the ruling, for the restriction is imposed in order to prevent the introduction of rabies. The law does not apply in the United States,

Left
It is rare for cats to enjoy walking on a lead but it is certainly possible to train them to accept a collar and walk calmly on a lead if they are introduced to it as young kittens. This can be very useful at certain times, for instance on journeys and in cars.

Right
Kittens playing. Instinctively they use the fighting technique of all wild animals – the left kitten has forestalled an ambush and promptly caught his ambusher with a paw. He will next go for his neck in playful attack. Only full grown toms actually do each other damage.

but a certificate is required there to show that the cat is free from infection and that it has not been in contact with an animal carrying rabies. Quarantine regulations in Australia are as strict as in Britain.

Travelling with a cat
People who take their holidays in country cottages or in caravans have no such problems. Provided it has been trained to a lead since its early days as a kitten, a cat can be taken along with the family. This type of training should start at about three months. The kitten must be fitted with an elasticated collar to lessen the risk of injury if it is caught up while climbing trees or exploring the undergrowth. It will probably object at first, so the process should be a gradual one—a few minutes each day, increasing to rather longer periods. Once the collar is accepted without fuss, the lead can be attached, initially for a short time and then for progressively longer sessions.

It is essential to keep your cat under control when it is travelling in a car, and a lead is useful for this purpose. There are so many potential dangers if you allow it complete freedom. A sudden noise can alarm the animal so that it impedes the movements of the driver; or the car door could be opened inadver-

tently, causing the terrified cat to leap out in front of passing vehicles, risking its own life and perhaps bringing about an accident.

Another method of transport is in a specially designed travelling basket; but be particularly careful to see that it is securely fastened, for cats can be quite expert at sliding back hinges. The basket should be lined with clean newspaper and a warm blanket. For a short journey a simple hold-all can be used. Place the cat in the bag with the zip fastener closed, leaving only its head free so that he can see what is going on. On all occasions the odd word or caress will have a calming influence.

Moving house will also involve a journey for your pet. It is unlikely to be enthusiastic about the idea but if it has attached itself firmly to the family and if you take pains to reassure it, the change should not be difficult. On arrival, your cat may sulk at first and sit mulishly under the heaviest piece of furniture so that it cannot be reached or coaxed out. It may also refuse to eat and will almost certainly succeed in making you feel guilty for having removed it from familiar surroundings. After a little while, however, it will decide to explore the house, and will be puzzled by discovering new smells and recognizing

smells of carpets and furniture from the old home at the same time.

Reassured, your pet will settle down for a wash, and this is a signal that it is ready to eat. Do not try to hurry the programme but let it follow its course. Like you, the cat has new territory to explore and claim. Provide a litter tray and keep the animal in the house for a day or two until it has adjusted.

One old practice when moving house was to butter the cat's paws, which may have served a useful purpose if only to keep it occupied cleaning the butter off and giving it no time to be nervous. It is doubtful whether there is any other benefit. Should your cat be missing in spite of all your precautions, the first place to look is back at the previous address. Cats have been known to travel considerable distances to return to their old homes.

Safety measures

Cats are all too frequently found lying mutilated or dead by the roadside, for today's fast motoring takes a sad toll of our pets. If you live in a town or near a motorway it is essential to keep an animal under the strictest control and vigilance. If your cat has been trained to the lead it can be taken out under super-

vision. If you have a garden close to a highway a wired-in exercise area should be provided. The wire must, of course, cover the top as well, as a cat is an expert escapologist. In a flat a balcony is not suffi-cient as a place of exercise nor, unless enclosed, is it safe, because another danger for a cat is height. It is an old wives' tale that a cat always lands on its feet. Certainly it has a well developed sense of balance and can often right itself as it falls. Its natural grace and suppleness will frequently come to its rescue when another animal would meet certain death; but even so, the cat is not immortal and its tiny bones may easily be broken.

Two or three years ago in Glasgow a large number of cats were unaccountably being injured over a short period as a result of falls. The theory put forward by the P.D.S.A. was that during this particular time there was an abundance of thistledown in the air. In their attempts to reach it as it floated high above the city, the playful animals simply tumbled from win-dowsills. Cat owners were therefore warned to be on their special guard.

Should your cat have the misfortune to injure itself, it must be kept warm and quiet, and veterinary help should be called immediately. My own cat broke

Cats usually know how to make themselves comfortable and these kittens have found an unusual and warm spot to sleep beneath a radiator where they can feel secure and protected.

a leg after falling from an apple tree where she had climbed in pursuit of birds. Fortunately, professional treatment soon put her right and there were no ill effects after the bones had knit.

Town life has many hazards but even the country cat is not entirely without risk, for there is a danger from poison by swallowing weedkiller or by eating a small animal which has itself been poisoned.

The problem of strays

When a hungry, bedraggled waif of a cat appears on the doorstep begging for food, it is hard to resist. But although your instinct is to take it in and cosset it until it looks as sleek and well fed as your own cat, resist the temptation or you may be introducing infection to your family pet. Before inviting the stranger to share your hearth and home you must have it examined by the vet to make sure it is not carrying disease. Meanwhile you can feed it in the garage or somewhere outside the house until you have made the necessary arrangements. If a stray decides to adopt you, do make sure that it belongs to nobody else, for the real owner will obviously be distressed by its absence. It has been known for cats to keep

two homes going and even answer to two names, but you must be careful not to fall victim to such a confidence trick!

You can help to make sure that you are not adding to the already serious overpopulation problem by having your own cat altered at a suitable age, assuming you do not want it for breeding. The operation, both for a male and a female, is a simple affair for your vet, and all cats are improved thereby, especially a tom, who will be less likely to want to stay out at night. Rossini wrote a very amusing duet simulating the wailing of courting cats, which, by virtue of considerable artistic licence, was made to sound melodious. It is far less amusing when this caterwauling takes place under your window in the early hours of the morning. Neutering of your male will hopefully dispense with such an experience, apart from bringing other advantages inside the home; and spaying a female may avoid the grievous necessity of having kittens put to sleep.

Having observed the basic rules mentioned in this chapter at the beginning of your new relationship, you will soon discover the many delights of sharing your home with a cat.

Left
An Abyssinian eating grass. It is very important to provide a pot of grass for any cat who is confined to a building.

Below
Comfort and company in front of the fire.

Siamese and other Foreign Breeds

Mary Dunnill

Left
Two young champion
Seal Point Siamese.

Following page left
A beautiful Lilac Point
Siamese admiring herself
in a mirror. The
character of a Lilac Point
is calmer and gentler
than that of other
Siamese. Their
temperament seems to be
in keeping with their
delicate shading. In
America this cat is
known as the Frost
Point.

Following page below
A Lilac Point Siamese
and a Blue Point
Siamese. These cats
dislike the cold and
appreciate a well made
basket with a comfortable
warm blanket. They
always look a little
exotic out of doors and
are rarely able to find
any camouflage when
they hunt birds and mice.

Two medals have recently come into my hands, one won by Lady Vyvyan for Best Two Kittens in Class 20 at the 20th Cat Show held at the Crystal Palace in 1888, the other by Miss Forestier-Walker for Best Cat in Classes 7–15 at the 25th Annual Cat Show at the Crystal Palace in 1893. These two ladies were among the original importers of Siamese cats; they brought a Siamese male and female and a pair of kittens home to England in 1886 from the Far East and no doubt these medals were won by progeny of these cats.

It is generally accepted that the Siamese cat is of Eastern origin and is often referred to as an Oriental, together with the Abyssinian and the Burmese. Today Oriental is being used as an umbrella-name, covering Foreign Shorthaired cats and all the new varieties derived from the Siamese; but since the name has not yet been given official blessing, we have Foreign White, Foreign Lilac, Foreign Black and so on. Numerically however, the Siamese cats and the Burmese cats are still the most important of the Orientals.

The Siamese

Early records of Siamese in England refer to two types, the Royal Cat of Siam whose body is 'of a dun colour, nose, part of the face, ears, feet and tail of a very dark chocolate brown, nearly black, eyes of a beautiful blue by day and of a red colour at night'. The other type, the chocolate, is 'of a very rich chocolate or seal, with darker face, ears and tail; the legs are a shade darker, which intensifies towards the feet. The eyes of a rich amber colour'. It could be that these chocolates were, in fact, Burmese/Siamese hybrids but at that time the Burmese, as a breed, had not been named as such. Harrison Weir comments that the grey or fawn colour, with black and well-marked muzzle, ears and legs, is the typical variety, the markings being the same as those of Himalayan rabbits. It is this coat pattern that is the characteristic feature of the Siamese cat, whatever the variety.

Whether Seal Point, Blue Point, Tabby Point, etc., the colour is always restricted to the points.

Many of the early cats had a kink in the tail, sometimes almost a hook. There were bob-tails, too, and one very famous stud cat had a short, stumpy tail. Today we look for a long whip-like tail and only a small, almost imperceptible kink at the end of the tail is permissible. However, there are many people who regard the kink and the crossed-eye as characteristics of the Siamese and deplore the endeavours to breed them out.

The appearance of the Siamese cat has changed in the ninety-odd years since the first two, Pho and Mia, arrived in England. Pictures of the early cats show a rather round head, with smallish ears. The present day Siamese cat has a long wedge-shaped head, long, lean body, long legs and a long tail. It is an elegant, beautiful creature, graceful in movement, with vivid blue, almond-shaped eyes. The unusual coat pattern and inscrutable expression makes this a 'cat with a difference'.

The Seal Point, with points of dark brown and a cream body colour, is the best known and most popular variety. For many years Blue Point were regarded as freaks or sports, but 'very lovely animals with the palest of cream coats and lavender blue points. Sometimes the points are of a stone grey colour, which detracts from their beauty'. One wonders if the so-called lavender blue could have been what today is the Lilac Point. The Chocolate Point has points of milk-chocolate colour whereas the Seal Point's colour is plain chocolate. There are now Red Points, Cream Points, Tabby Points in all colours (Seal, Blue, Chocolate, Lilac and Red), and Tortoiseshell Points all officially recognized as varieties of Siamese. Smoke Siamese and the Pastel Tabby Points have not yet received an official blessing.

Siamese kittens are born white, and there is the story of a novice breeder who put down a litter of

Right
A young Tortie Point
Siamese cat. These are
sometimes laughed at for
their strange markings,
but they have very
sweet temperaments
and are particularly
useful to the serious
Siamese breeder as
they have evenly patched
points and are usually of
beautiful type. Mated
to a basic colour they
can produce all the
various points.

Below right
A beautiful Tabby Point
Siamese. These cats are
'show stoppers' with
their well ringed tails
with solid black tips and
black stockings up the
backs of their hind legs.

kittens, thinking her queen had mismated, when no characteristic coat pattern was seen. The first sign of colour is a faint pencil line on the edge of the ears. The dark brown of the Seal Points is relatively quick to show, though sometimes the Seals have a blueish tinge. It is difficult to distinguish between Chocolate, Lilac and Blue in a mixed litter. Sometimes the colour of the nose leather or paw pads will help one to decide, but this is not infallible. Ideally, whatever the colour, all the points should match. It is particularly difficult to achieve this with the Red Points and the Chocolate Points. All Siamese cats should have blue eyes, though the exact shade of blue can vary with the various points' colours.

Seal Points, Blue Points, Chocolate Points and Lilac Points are all classified as the same breed, with separate subdivisions according to colour. The Tabby Points ('their mother a wandering Siamese, their father a travelling man') and the Tortie Points are classified in a separate breed. They, too, come in all the afore-mentioned colours and with the introduction of orange a considerable number of variations are added to the breed. Recently, Silver (Chinchilla) has been introduced, giving us Smokes and Pastels in all colours.

Siamese cats are prolific breeders and are good mothers. An average litter is five kittens, but there are instances of ten or even twelve kittens being reared, with assistance perhaps from a foster-mother or nurse cat. One of my own queens, with her first litter, reared eight kittens, feeding them in two sittings, four at a time. For the most part, the male takes little or no part in the rearing of kittens, but an interesting story is recorded in an American cat magazine of a Siamese Champion who was devoted to a certain queen—Champion Miskin. When the latter was nearly due to kitten he started to make a bed by deliberately plucking himself, pulling large tufts of hair from his tail and haunches. He placed these tufts with great care on a large round cushion, beginning with a circular outer rim, gradually working towards the centre until a luxurious nest had been completed. He would then grab his mate by the neck and place her on the bed, talking to her for hours. When the kittens arrived he showed evident signs of pleasure, placing them on his cushion and waiting for more to arrive.

Breeding should not be undertaken unless one has the proper facilities—plenty of space, time and patience. The voice of a Siamese queen in season is unbelievably raucous and can be very nerve-racking. An entire male needs to be confined in his own stud quarters. He should not be allowed to roam in search of wives, but should not be so isolated as to become lonely.

The Siamese cat is highly intelligent and easily trained. It is very demanding of love and attention, likes to converse, and makes a wonderful companion; and since it is not happy left alone, the best notion is to have a pair, or even more! But one cannot generalize about the Siamese. Each is an individual, telling you how he wishes to be treated, demanding to be loved, petted and played with, expecting you to understand what he says, and giving you, in return, his deep devotion.

The American-bred Burmese

The Burmese cat is, in most respects, like the Siamese. In America, as recently as 1949, Doris Bryant wrote that 'very dark Siamese are sometimes called Chocolate Siamese and sometimes they are called Burmese'. It is probable that the 'other type (of Siamese), the Chocolate, of a very rich chocolate or seal, with darker face, ears, tail and legs; eyes of a rich amber colour', imported into England with the first 'dun-coloured Siamese', were in fact hybrids from crosses between Siamese and an un-named dark-coated cat. In many of the early books about cats the name Burmese was applied to the cat we now call Birman, or the Sacred Cat of Burma, but this breed is very different from our present-day Burmese cat. In 1927, Mrs French's Granny Grumps, herself all-brown, was mated to a Seal Point and produced a hybrid, Timkey

Browne, who himself sired a litter of brown kittens which were exhibited at the Siamese Cat Club's 5th Show. 'We were rather struck by Mrs French's brown kittens and think this variety well worth developing. They are quite different from the chocolates, their colour being much that of a Havana cigar, with darker points. If the colour can be fixed and better eye colour obtained, we have here a very pretty and uncommon-looking cat.' (Cat Gossip, 1928.)

The Burmese breed as we know it today was made in U.S.A., not in Britain. In 1930 Dr Joseph C. Thompson took a brown cat named Wong Mau from Burma to America. She herself was a hybrid from Siamese and a dark-coated breed named Burmese. Mated to a Siamese, she produced hybrids and Siamese. When the Burmese/Siamese hybrids were mated together, the darker coated Burmese were produced. These bred true, and in 1936 the Burmese was officially recognized in the United States of America as a new show breed. However, official recognition was withdrawn in 1947 in an attempt to control the breeding and to stop hybrids being exhibited and sold as pure-bred Burmese. Full status for the Brown Burmese was restored in 1953, due to

Below
A Brown Burmese basking in the sunshine. Cats have an uncanny ability to find the warmest spot in which to sit. This cat has the typical coat of the Burmese with a high glossy sheen on it.

Right
A Cream Burmese and below a Blue Burmese. Burmese are great individualists and it is impossible to generalize about their characters. Every Burmese will have its own definite personality and will make a wonderful companion, and indeed demand to be taken as a serious member of the family.

the work of the Burmese Cat Society of America.

The first pure-bred Burmese cats were imported into England from America by Mrs Lilian France in 1949. These were Champion Laos Cheli Wat and Chindwin's Minou Twm, both females, and a male, Casa Gatos da Foong. Another male, Casa Gatos Darkee arrived in 1953. These early Burmese, like the first Siamese to come to England, did not take kindly to our climate and were chesty and delicate. I well remember seeing one of the first Burmese kittens bred by Mrs France and owned by Miss Lant of Loughborough, who gave me my first Siamese kitten. The little Burmese was a pathetic mite, wheezy and full of snuffles; I much preferred my Siamese kitten Beaumanor Becky. However, as the cats became acclimatized, their stamina improved and today, generally speaking, Burmese cats are tough and very healthy. Mrs France passed this stock to Mr and Mrs V. Watson, who imported another unrelated male, Darshan Khudiran, from America in 1957.

The Brown Burmese has a rich, dark seal-brown body colour, shading to a slightly lighter colour on the chest and belly; no decided contrast of points and body colour should be evident. Young adults and older kittens may be slightly lighter and show greater contrast; young kittens generally are lighter and may show ghost tabby markings which will disappear later. White hairs (indicating white-spotting) are undesirable, and a white patch, as with white toes in Siamese, is not permissible. The general type is similar to the Siamese cat, the body being medium sized, not so long as a Siamese but not cobby, svelte, with a slender neck, slim legs and oval paws; the hind legs should be slightly longer than the front, giving a slight tilt from the horizontal to the back level. The tail is long but should not be whip-like. The face is wedge-shaped but shorter, blunter and wider at the jaw than Siamese. The skull should be rounded and the profile shows a break at the top of the nose. The chin should be firm and a jaw pinch is a fault. The ears should be large, continuing the line of the wedge-shaped face, wide at the base and slightly rounded at the tip. The eyes should be a golden yellow, wide apart and almond-shaped. Green or blue-green eyes are a fault. The coat should be short, fine-textured and close-lying, with a high glossy sheen.

The Blue Burmese was the first unexpected colour to arrive. In 1955, Chinki Golden Gay (Chinki is Mrs France's prefix) was mated back to her father, Casa Gatos Darkee, and produced a litter of four kittens, one of which was much lighter than the other three. As this kitten grew, her coat colour became a bluish grey. She was registered as Sealcoat Blue Surprise. By 1960 breeders had succeeded in establishing three generations of blue-to-blue matings, and sought official recognition from the Governing Council of the Cat Fancy, this being granted in June 1960. Since then many colour variations have been added to the Brown

58

and Blue varieties. There are now Cream, Blue-Cream, Red, Tortie, Chocolate (Champagne in America) and Lilac (Platinum) Burmese.

At the National Cat Club Show at Olympia, in 1974, at which I was show manager for the Shorthair section, there were no less than ninety kittens entered in the Any Colour Burmese Kitten Class offered by the Burmese Cat Club. This club, very properly, will not allow Burmese kittens to be entered in shows under the age of three calendar months, not even in litters. The club caters for all the colours of Burmese, and from small beginnings in 1954 is now second in numbers to the Siamese Cat Club, and very strong in unity of purpose.

The Burmese cat is affectionate and demonstrative, loving human companionship. It is high-spirited and quite irrepressible. I know one wicked little female that can squeeze through the letter-box to get out. She will then rush to the top of a tall pine tree and cry to be rescued. She has never learned how to clamber down and enjoys the trouble she causes.

The Havana
The Havana is also an all-brown Shorthaired cat of Foreign type, basically a self-brown Siamese with no visible signs whatsoever of the Siamese coat pattern. Brown cats are mentioned in the early literature, 'Mrs Herbert Young's chocolate Fatima, imported, won First Prize, Pulborough 1888, supposed to be the only Chocolate Siamese in Europe'. Major Woodiwiss

registered Wendie and Wander in 1921, Wendie a pointed Siamese, Wander a Chocolate Siamese. Their dam was Winkie and the sire, Chocolate Cream; both these cats had identical ancestors – imported cats, 'particulars unknown'. Wander won a First Prize at Croydon Show in 1923. Sister Stockley's Adastra won First Prize in the Chocolate Class at the Siamese Cat Club Show in 1925. Mrs French's afore-mentioned Timkey Browne was born on 16 August, 1927 and registered with his litter sisters, Dido and Cora Capps, as Seal Point Siamese. Their dam was Granny Grumps, an imported all-brown cat, their sire Champion Bonzo. Timkey Browne was different – born the colour of café-au-lait, not white. In 1928, he won a special prize for best body colour in the same class as his litter sister Dido, who became a famous Champion Seal Point; and he sired the litter of brown kittens shown at the Siamese Cat Club's 5th Show, whose colour was described as being much that of a Havana cigar, with darker points. The late Mrs Kent once told me that Mrs French 'knew an awful lot, all about the Selfs all these newcomers think they have invented. They were there but not recognized or admitted to shows'. It is reasonable to think that many of these brown cats were what today would be termed Siamese/Burmese hybrids.

The Havana, as we know it nowadays, is a manufactured breed, the end result of a planned programme for the breeding of a self-brown cat of Foreign type. In the 1950s, five lines were started. Miss Von Ullman

Left
The Havana, a manufactured breed which is basically a self-coloured Brown Siamese but with no sign of the Siamese coat pattern. They have green eyes as opposed to the yellow eyes of the Burmese and the face shape is similar to that of a Siamese rather than to the more wedged shape face of the Burmese.

Right
A Foreign White kitten. This is the one self-colour cat of Siamese type which has proved difficult to breed true.

(Roofspringer) mated a black cat to her Chocolate Point stud Siamese, Mrs Hargreaves (Laurentide) crossed a Russian Blue hybrid, Laurentide Aretoo Pearl with Mrs Fisher's Chocolate Point, Briarry Saccharin. Mrs Fisher (Praha) had Laurentide Arduo Prizm, a black/Russian hybrid and mated her to a Chocolate Point. Mrs Monro-Smith (Elmtower) mated a black queen from a mongrel mating of her Chocolate Point back to her Siamese grandfather. Mrs Judd started an outcross line, with her prefix Crossways. Mrs Dora Clarke mated a Seal Point queen, Our Miss Smith, to Elmtower Bronze Idol and produced Craigiehilloch Bronze Leaf and Craigiehilloch Bronze Wing. The 1960s saw several more breeders and new prefixes—Mrs Warren (Senlac), Mr Scott (Bluetower), Mrs Dunnill (Sumfun), Mrs Kirby (Crumberhill) and Mrs Stewart (Sweethope). The 1970s have brought many new enthusiasts to the breed and many new prefixes appear among the prize winners on the show bench—Dandycat Brown Bear, Florentine M'Bele, Kalaya Butterscotch, Samsara Saburi, Scintilla Copper Beech, Siavana Feu Follette and Solitaire Maneki

Neko, to name just a few.

The breed was granted official recognition in 1958 under the name Chestnut Brown (Foreign). This name certainly describes the coat colour aimed at by all breeders of this cat, a warm ruddy brown like a ripe conker, but it was clumsy and we were all pleased when, in 1971, the official name was changed to Havana. This cat should have a long, well-proportioned head narrowing to a fine muzzle, the ears large, wide at the base, with good width between. The eyes are green. The body should be long and lithe, legs slim, paws oval. The tail is long and whip-like, with no kink. The coat may be any shade of rich chestnut brown, short, glossy, even and sound throughout. Any tendency to black is penalized. Nose leather matches the coat colour but the paw pads should be pink.

The Havana is very intelligent, full of character, with a charming nature. His voice is quiet and he is a happy, healthy and playful cat, a wonderful companion and a joy to watch. I have been very fond of all the Havanas I have known.

Below
A famous family bred to create the Egyptian Mau already recognized in the USA. A female Havana carrying the Blue and Siamese factors was mated to a Chocolate Tabby Point carrying the Blue factor. They produced two foreign Lilacs, one Havana (later to be a champion), one Lilac Havana and one Chocolate Point Siamese, as well as the new Bronze and Lilac Egyptian Mau kittens.

Right
The Korat cat has a blue-grey coat with green eyes.

Recent introductions

The most recent Foreign Shorthairs to be elevated from the Any Other Variety category are the Foreign Lilacs and the Foreign Whites. The Foreign Lilac is genetically similar to the Siamese Lilac Point. Both parents must have the two genes, chocolate and blue, but they lack the gene restricting the colour to the points. Self Lilacs were produced by the Laurentide line in the 1950s, but, as I remember them, they were much paler and pinker in coat colour. Type is today much better and the Foreign Lilac, with sparkling green eyes, is a most attractive addition to the Show Bench.

The Foreign White is also a manufactured breed, a coloured cat of Siamese type, wearing a white overcoat. The breed has been built up by very careful matings with first-class Siamese for several generations. It began in 1962 when Miss Elizabeth Flack in Ireland, Miss Patricia Turner and Mr Brian Stirling-Webb decided to develop the idea of a blue-eyed white cat of Foreign type. Mr Stirling-Webb had crossed a non-pedigree white cat with his Seal-pointed

stud in his Rex breeding programme, and I suggested that he used this white hybrid to establish a white breed similar to the Havana. Miss Turner had a similar idea after studying some over-exposed photographs of her Lilac Point queen which made it look like a pure white Siamese. Miss Flack's Seal Point queen had mismated and produced three white kittens, one a blue-eyed female, and she decided to breed from her; so El Maharanee Saengdao became the foundation queen of the Irish line. Mr Stirling-Webb promised me the first blue-eyed female white that he bred, but I had to wait until 1966 for Briarry Venus Improved, for until then all the blue-eyed white cats had been males.

By 1965 eight breeders were actively involved in carefully formulated breeding programmes, and a provisional standard of points was drawn up. Very careful records were kept and only the very best white offspring used for breeding; the inevitable non-white kittens were neutered. Deafness, head smudges, long coarse coats, poor eye colour and odd eyes were some of the problems and defects that were encountered. The Foreign White today has achieved a high degree of perfection, but there are still stumbling blocks to be overcome. Breeding stock is carefully graded, and test matings establish the colours that the cats carry under their white overcoats. The lines that are red or tortie underneath are classed in a separate category and must only be bred under controlled conditions. They are not approved for white to white matings. They may be upgraded if the red complex can be bred out, but this can be a very lengthy process. A very careful breeding policy is laid down and the goal of establishing a fertile, pure breeding white cat free from inherited defects is still in the future. Meanwhile, more and more of these beautiful cats are seen and greatly admired.

Still to be officially recognized are the Foreign Blacks, Foreign Blues, Foreign Tabbies and Egyptian Mau. They are essentially the same in type and are derived from crosses with Siamese. All are very attractive, elegant cats and can be seen at most shows, either on exhibition or competing in the Any Other Variety classes.

The Foreign White, Foreign Lilac and other self-coloured cats that are derived from the Siamese are very similar to them in temperament, but perhaps a little quieter and less demanding. They are very intelligent, amiable, well aware of their beauty and elegance, and always ready to be admired.

The Korat is a silver-blue cat with green-gold eyes. Its origin is believed to be the Malay Self-Blue and is thought by some to have had a hand in the making of the Blue Point Siamese. A pair of Korats were imported into America in 1959, direct from Thailand, followed by others. A band of enthusiasts formed the Korat Cat Fanciers' Association in 1965 to look after the interests of the breed, and very strict conditions of ownership are enforced. Breeding is closely guarded

and is documented in detail. The breed is officially recognized in America, and is permitted to compete for show honours and championships there.

A small number of Korats have been brought to England from America but they have not yet received official blessing and a breed number.

The attractive Abyssinian
The Abyssinian is one of the oldest breeds of cats. It looks very much like the cats portrayed in ancient Egyptian wall paintings, but whether it actually originated in Abyssinia or Egypt has always been questioned. Many hold that it is a man-made breed from our native British Tabbies. It is a very beautiful cat, Foreign in type, with a long, lithe body, a long pointed head with large 'listening' ears, and almond-shaped eyes, green, yellow or hazel in colour. The feet are small with black pads, and black extends up the hind legs. The outstanding characteristic of this breed is the unique ticked coat, giving the cat a typical jungle appearance. Each hair has two or three distinct bands of colour, giving an effect similar to the coat of a hare; in fact, it has sometimes been called a bunny-cat or hare-cat. The colour of the standard or normal cat should be ruddy brown, ticked with black or dark brown. The inside of the forelegs and belly should harmonize with the main colour, preferably orange-brown. There should be no bars or markings on the body and legs or rings on the tail, but a dark spine line may be permitted. No white markings are allowed and a white chin is undesirable. It is an active, friendly cat and very intelligent. Not very prolific and somewhat of a rarity, it has been called 'Child of the Gods'.

There is a red variety, differing only in coat colour, which should be a rich copper red, with belly and inside of the legs a deep apricot. The nose leather and paw pads are pink and the dark extension up the back of the hind legs becomes dark brown. The spine line also is brown. The Red Abyssinian was given an official breed number in 1963. There is also now the Blue Abyssinian, officially recognized in England in 1974. Blue Abyssinians had been bred in California from normal Abyssinians in 1964 and, as with the Blue Burmese, was a surprise, not a planned introduction of a different colour. In England in 1963, Fairlie Mehesso and his brother Fairlie Menelic, both blue Abyssinians, were exhibited. In the fullness of time, Mehesso was mated to one of Mrs Evely's normal Abyssinian queens and a litter of two blue females, two blue males and a red male was produced, proving that the queen also carried the recessive blue gene. Here was the beginning of a new variety. No doubt there will be cream and lilac Abyssinian cats calling for breed numbers soon. To my mind, the beauty of the Blue Abyssinian is out of this world and I would dearly love to possess one.

The Abyssinian cat is devoted to its owner and somewhat of a one-person pet. I knew a male that

Previous page below right
A handsome Russian
Blue cat sometimes
known as the Chartreuse.

The Abyssinian. Although a superb creature, resembling his big cousin, the lion, this Abyssinian has faults — a white chin, white whiskers, and the faint markings of an 'M' on his forehead.

62

Left
A Blue Burmese.

Below left
The Red Abyssinian. In the United States, this cat is known as the 'Sorrel'. The type is very similar to the cats illustrated in Egyptian paintings and some people believe the Abyssinian may be a descendant of the sacred cat of Ancient Egypt. This cat is a good example of the type and the coat colour is true. Abyssinians are 'one man' cats; they talk a lot and can and will learn to retrieve objects thrown to them. As a general rule, they have small litters with seldom more than four kittens and more of them are male than female.

Right
An unusual cat – a Russian Blue or Chartreuse crossed with Siamese. This cat shows the wedged shape face of the true Russian Blue, and also the typical brilliant green, almond shaped eyes. A cat collar with the address attached is a wise idea if you live in a town or where the cat may stray or get lost. For cats living in the country, it is not so necessary and might even be dangerous if the collar catches on a branch and pulls the cat up sharply.

Left
A Blue-Cream dilute Cornish Rex cat. Notice how every hair is curly, even on the face and whiskers. Breeders have become increasingly fascinated by Blue-Cream cats. The Longhaired Blue-Cream cats are invariably female, and a definite formula has been worked out by the geneticists for breeding from Blues and Creams so that the offspring are predictable in colour.

Right
A Cream Cornish Rex cat posing half way up a tree. Rex cats have a devoted following and are generally hardy cats with very lively and individual personalities.

always swore most fiercely at me but was extremely gentle and affectionate with his owner. He was a hunter and would often bring home his kill, frequently a rabbit. Although given complete freedom, he always returned home on the dot for mealtimes.

The Russian Blue

The Russian Blue is a cat with a long body, graceful in outline and carriage, with a medium strong bone structure. The tail is fairly long and tapering. The head is short, wedge-shaped with a flat skull; forehead and nose are straight, forming an angle. Whisker pads are prominent. Eyes are vivid green, almond-shaped and set rather wide apart. The ears are long and pointed, wide at the base, set vertically to the head. The true Russian coat should be really short, thick and very fine, like plush. Any tendency to lie flat is wrong.

This breed has suffered much over the years from careless breeding and controversy. The cats have been known by many names—Archangel Blue, Spanish, Maltese, Foreign, Chartreuse, and American Blue. The worst damage to the breed was done when Siamese crosses were made, and a kind of self-blue Siamese was produced. A new standard of points was even drawn up in 1950 to accommodate the new Russian, and some of the cats pictured in current literature still show the results. Fortunately, however, in 1965 the standard was re-written, returning approximately to the old standard, and a real effort is being made internationally to get back the original kind of cat. The best Russians in England were bred by Marie Rochford and her Dunloe prefix is world famous. The Russian Blue Association, founded in 1967, is guiding breeders of this attractive cat, and it is hoped that we shall see increasing numbers.

The Russian Blue is a hardy cat, preferring an outdoor life. Somewhat aloof and rather silent, with a small voice, it is nevertheless good-tempered, affectionate and intelligent.

The Cornish and Devon Rex

In 1950, an unusual curly-coated kitten was born in a Cornish farm cat's litter. The owner, having owned Rex rabbits, called it a Rex cat, and with the help of progressive fanciers began to establish it as a new breed. As far as was known at the time, this exciting mutation was a unique occurrence in the history of cat breeding. The cat is of modified Foreign type with a wedge-shaped head, and can be bred in all coat colours.

Eleven years later, another curly kitten of uncommon Foreign appearance was born in the neighbouring county of Devon. Coming so comparatively soon after the emergence of Cornish Rex, it was assumed that the two events were related. Test matings, however, proved conclusively that they were the result of two separate genes, and both Devon Rex, as it came to be called, and Cornish Rex were eventually added to the list of recognized breeds.

Feline First Aid

Michael Findlay

Left
The cat is potentially 'a well equipped fighting unit'. This comical Silver Tabby illustrates this perfectly:– a fine set of teeth and four sets of claws all at the ready, although he is so held as to be off balance. A blow from a cat's front paw can be very powerful.

Right
This cuddly kitten looks as if butter wouldn't melt in its mouth. However at the merest suspicion of 'treatment' he will move like lightning and his loose fitting coat will make it very difficult for you to hold on to him at all. These are the cats' natural protections against examination of any kind.

Following page left
A patient green-eyed Tabby wrapped up in a towel which is a good way of restricting the cat's movements if you have to treat him on your own.

Of the many species that have been domesticated over the years, the cat is, in many ways, one of the most complex. Brave and fearless, as befits its wild ancestry, the popular household pet retains the habits and behaviour of its jungle relatives. As a result, veterinary treatment of the cat poses a number of specific problems.

Day in, day out, the veterinarian hears from his clients the well-worn cliché, . . . but they can't talk!' This remark misses the point completely – of course cats cannot talk in the human sense, but they *can* communicate to a surprising extent to an experienced person. To the veterinary surgeon, who is trained to diagnose, administer to, treat and nurse 'dumb' patients on the premise of acting basically on facts gleaned from keen observation and questioning of the owner, this is of paramount importance. Experience may, therefore, give the vet a pretty good idea of what is wrong with a sick cat; but obviously other aids (such as X-rays, tests on blood, urine, etc) will be employed, in addition to routine clinical examination, before a diagnostic conclusion is reached and suitable treatment chosen.

The cat as patient

Carrying the analogy between cats and human patients a stage further, what is of far greater practical importance is the absence of co-operation. The average cat tends to dislike examination and treatment, for it cannot comprehend that what is being done is for its own good. Its instinctive reaction, when being forced to do something undesirable, is to resist. Even the most compliant domestic pet is, potentially. a well-equipped 'fighting unit'. In addition to a battery of fearsome teeth, the average cat has four lethal claws on each hind foot and five on each front foot. It also possesses a loose-fitting coat which enables it to swivel through wide angles within the skin itself, so

69

that the handler is often at risk. Although the paws can be immobilized, there is little to prevent a cat biting. So it may be necessary, both in the veterinary surgery and the home, to employ custom-built methods for restraining the feline patient for purposes of examination and treatment.

For the single-handed operative, the best method is to wrap the body of the cat, including all four limbs, in a large blanket or towel. Alternatively, the animal can be enclosed, except for the head, in a zip-up bag. If an assistant is present, the task is, of course, much easier. The cat is placed on a table or on the knee of the assistant who holds the front legs, allowing the vet control of the animal's head. But with a really difficult patient two assistants may be required to keep the cat under sufficient restraint for the surgeon to go about his work without fear of being molested.

An additional problem is the natural inclination of

the cat to interfere with surgical procedures and thus undo whatever good has been done. The patient obviously cannot be kept under observation day and night, nor can it be expected to respond to human words of advice. After all, even a child will pay heed to the warning, 'Don't pick it, or it will never get better'. Yet considering the number of operations performed daily on cats, they are, on the whole, obliging patients. Probably only one cat in fifty removes its stitches a few hours after they have been carefully inserted.

Because of the cat's shape and suppleness, it is almost impossible to bandage it in such a way that it cannot interfere with a wound, but there are three useful tips that may avoid yet another telephone call to the vet. Firstly, a bland, safe but unpleasant-tasting lotion, such as oil of citronella, can be painted *around* a lesion or wound, and this may discourage the cat

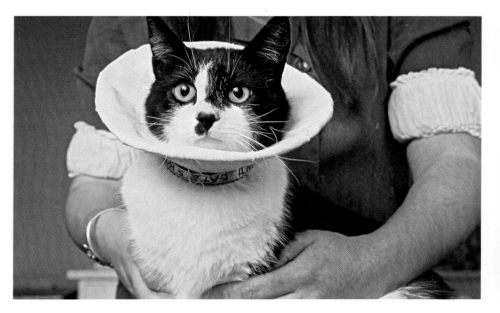

from licking it; but it is not foolproof, for the cat, being fastidiously clean, may be spurred to rid its skin of the noxious material. Secondly, bandaging the back paws with children's socks, for example, will, if the cat is detained indoors, lessen the risk of claws scratching out stitches or dressings applied to any point from the chest forward—and hence within reasonable range of the rear limbs. Thirdly, there is the classic 'Elizabethan collar'—a cone of cardboard or other suitable material around the neck, ensuring that the scratching *and* licking capabilities of the patient are severely restricted. Take care that this is the right size and not too tight—if in doubt seek advice from your vet or from his nursing staff.

A cat recovering from a broken limb, however, presents rather more of a practical problem. Whether the limb has been treated by means of an external plaster cast or with a stainless steel pin inserted through the bone itself, damage rarely occurs and the cat seldom interferes. Furthermore, being a sensible creature, the cat will bear little or no weight on an uncomfortable or painful limb—such as might be expected in the first stages of healing—and will

Above
Cat in an 'Elizabethan collar' which prevents him from licking a wound and also from biting and scratching you.

Right
Even a tiny kitten has a fierce battery of claws which he will use without hesitation. You can teach your kitten to retract his claws when playing with you and if you do have to 'doctor' him later it is possible that he will still not scratch you.

Below
The country cat is exposed to barbed wire, drains and even dead branches in trees, and accidents can occasionally happen.

resume normal mobility only when discomfort ceases and the limb has mended.

Home nursing

The most important role that an owner will occasionally be asked to play is that of home nurse. This may involve administering medicines, as directed by the vet. As a general rule, it is not advisable to mix medicines with food, in the hope that the patient will swallow it down unnoticed. The cat, being a fastidious and cautious feeder, is extremely suspicious of 'doctored grub' and unlikely to take all or indeed any of a treated meal or drink, so that the dosage, often critical, cannot be calculated with accuracy. For this reason drugs are rarely given now in powder form. Tablets or pills must be given exactly as instructed,

a wound in this manner.

Any cat with an orthopaedic complaint, a highly infectious condition, or in a generally weakened state, should *not* be allowed outdoors, or at least only if accompanied, for obvious reasons. If in doubt, ask the vet whether it is necessary to impose house arrest in the course of treatment; and if the answer is yes, do remember to provide an indoor litter tray.

As with human nursing, you will be expected to keep an eye on the patient and report progress. Obviously you will get in touch with your vet should there be signs of complications or deterioration; but do so, if only to obtain reassurance, should you be in the slightest doubt.

A word about force-feeding. It is far better for a cat to eat of its own free will than have to be forcibly

Opposite page
A Seal Colourpoint. The long hair can sometimes hide injuries and once they have been discovered may have to be cut away so that the wound can be treated.

Left
Giving a cat a pill. This is the correct way to hold the cat's head once you have secured his paws. Open the mouth by gently easing down the lower jaw with finger and

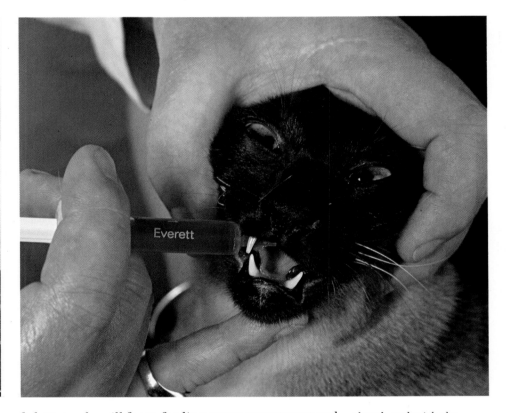

with regard both to intervals between dosages and to feeding times. Provided the cat is satisfactorily immobilized, it is not difficult to administer them, although it is important to see that the cat has finally swallowed the pill and not hidden it under his tongue.

Liquid medicines may be given in drop form with an eye-dropper (fountain pen filler) or the barrel of a hypodermic syringe, which can be obtained from your vet. The principle is the same as with pills, and it is reassuring to know that, given the cat's very strong throat reflexes, neither solid nor liquid medicines are likely to go down the wrong way.

Ointments, creams and the like may be applied, under suitable direction, but do remember that these can easily be licked off during the normal cleaning process. So try to prevent your pet doing this by keeping it under observation for a while after treating

fed. Not only will force-feeding create resentment and antipathy, but it must be done frequently and regularly. At best it will merely sustain life and energy, and it is impossible to force enough food down to build up the patient's strength. It is much preferable to encourage the cat to eat tasty, strongly flavoured foods, such as tinned sardines, salmon and tuna, raw liver and scraped raw beef—perhaps with a pinch of salt as an additional spur. Invariably, when a cat starts to eat following surgery or illness, it will go from strength to strength.

If, however, it proves necessary to force-feed for a temporary period, the vet will suggest appropriate foods. These may include essence of beef or chicken, glucose and milk, proprietary dried milk for cats, beef tea, human invalid diets and tinned baby foods. They should be given in fluid or paste form by the methods previously suggested.

thumb and with the other hand push the pill right to the back of the cat's throat. Cats are quite capable of holding the pill in their mouth for a long time and then spitting it out. Try to ensure that the cat has swallowed it before you let him go, by stroking his throat.

Above
A Siamese being fed with a pen filler; the principle is the same as with pills, but do not give him more than he can swallow at a time.

A comfortable environment, airy but draught free, and including direct heat by any safe method, is also an invaluable aid to nursing the really sick cat.

Finally, some warnings for the home nurse. On no account use old medicines unless sanctioned by your vet. Never use human medicines—even a minute dose of aspirin, for example, is enough to kill your cat. Be very cautious indeed about disinfectants, for a cat may die if it comes in contact with strong phenol preparations, which have little or no effect on other animals. Do not use insecticidal powders on a cat, unless specifically prescribed and guaranteed to be safe; insecticides containing DDT—much used until recently—can again prove fatal. And if you have access to morphine—a strictly controlled drug for human use—keep it well out of reach for this is an immediate killer.

Early visits to the surgery

It is probably true to say that the cat is one of the healthiest domestic species, particularly when treated with some knowledge, respect and forethought.

If you want a thoroughbred kitten, buy from a reputable breeder and try to see its first home and, if possible, its parents. Bear in mind the hidden extras to the purchase price, such as feeding, boarding, inoculations, neutering and possible veterinary fees (which can be cared for by taking out an insurance policy). Even when acquiring an ordinary 'moggie', go for one that is apparently healthy, playful, clean and alert. In either case you are within your rights to make your purchase conditional on a veterinary 'all-clear' within the first few days of acquisition.

Although always available to tender advice about buying kittens, a vet will normally see them for the first time at about nine weeks old, when they should be checked from head to toe and any minor problems remedied. At this stage we commonly give advice about exercise, grooming (at least once a day for *all* cats) and diet. It is important to remember that no cat in the wild ever lived on a staple diet of milk and fish, and that the same applies to the household pet. As with babies, the greater variety of food, the better, for this ensures that all essential vitamins, minerals,

etc are provided, with special supplements prescribed if and when they may be necessary.

One of the very common problems detected at this early stage is **parasitic otitis**—an inflammation of the ear canal caused by tiny parasitic mites. It is characterized by a copious amount of dark, crumbly wax, easily visible inside the ear flap and rather resembling peaty soil. Although of uncertain origin, the condition can be readily and permanently cured by means of specific ear drops, usually combined by cleansing of the ear by the vet. Parasitic otitis may be suspected if the kitten scratches its ears continuously. A healthy cat should have absolutely clean ears, with a slightly oily film, and if this is not the case, a visit to the vet is advisable. Do not, under any circumstances, poke any object into a cat's ear.

From about nine weeks of age kittens can, at the moment, be vaccinated against only one disease—**feline infectious enteritis**. This disease is not very common, but when it does occur it is highly infectious and, despite early diagnosis and speedy treatment, almost invariably fatal. It is caused by a virus which

*Previous page above
A Silver Tabby voices
his comments about a
routine ear inspection.
If you have any
suspicion that your cat
is troubled by his
ears it is best to go at
once to the vet.*

attacks the lining of stomach and bowel, resulting in vomiting, diarrhoea, dehydration (loss of fluids), collapse and death, often within a matter of hours. It is therefore recommended that all cats should be vaccinated, especially those attending cat shows, where a large number of animals are confined within a small area. All good boarding catteries will also refuse to accept a cat which has not been vaccinated against this disease. One or two injections may be required; they are painless and usually without side-effects. They should be boosted from time to time, as advised by the vet.

Treatment for roundworms, discussed later, should also be given at this stage.

Neutering and breeding

The second visit to the surgery, from five months onwards, is most frequently for the purpose of neutering the kitten. The operation of castrating a male kitten is straightforward – a form of routine surgery which most vets undertake daily. It involves a brief stay in the surgery, a short period under anaesthetic, and usually no return visit for stitch removal. There are three good reasons for recommending this operation on the male cat – to minimize the risk of battle scars and possible infections, to reduce the chances of road accidents in the course of sexual forays, and to modify the habit of spraying urine around the house.

Female cats should also be neutered (spayed) in order to prevent unwanted kittens. Cats rarely reach sexual maturity before the age of six months, so the operation can be planned in advance. Again it involves a short period in the surgery and under anaesthetic, although the operation (quite safe) is slightly longer and more complex than in the case of the male. The kitten will come home with some stitches in her flank or on her stomach, and these may, if not self-dissolving, have to be removed in the surgery a week later.

In neither case does the operation cause any discomfort to the tiny patient, there is little if any risk, and there is emphatically no cruelty involved. If done at an early age, there will be no change in the cat's temperament.

If you intend to breed from your queen kitten or if you are certain of being able to care for 'accidental' offspring, you must be aware of the cat's sexual cycle. From the age of about five to six months (but often not until eight or nine) a female cat is receptive to the male, will permit mating and will conceive. When in season she will 'call' (emitting a peculiar, low, throaty growl), show excessive affection both to humans and to other cats, and roll on her back, in addition to displaying other characteristic symptoms. It is unwise to allow a mating before the kitten has matured – say at one year old – for otherwise there may be kittening problems, draining the immature, growing queen of body reserves. Pregnancy varies within normal limits from 60–70 days, a convenient average for calculation being exactly nine weeks.

If you have a young Siamese Queen and want to breed from her it is important to remember that you must be able to look after any accidental off-spring and also that you have a responsibility to keep the breed pure. Cats are excellent mothers and their kittening should not be any problem to you – if there are complications it is best to call in the vet. The kittens' eyes will open when they are seven to ten days old and from then on they develop quickly. Keep the queen quiet, warm and with all the food she wants. At three to four weeks you can begin to introduce a milk mixture, and solids at about five to six weeks.

Left
Shorthaired Odd-eyed
White.

Right
Shorthaired Blue with
very clear yellow eyes.
Cats rarely experience
eye trouble but when
they do it should be
promptly treated.

Below
Healthy Chocolate Point
Siamese kittens in a
strong, draught free
basket.

Kittening is rarely complicated, but the owner should be well acquainted with normal behaviour so that veterinary help may be summoned should anything go wrong. Cats are generally very natural, attentive mothers, and it may be necessary to wean the kittens, so that they feed independently, if they have not volunteered to do so by the age of six weeks.

Standard health care

It is important to keep an eye on your cat's teeth after the age of, say, seven years. A hard chalky coating called tartar (or calculus) is deposited from the saliva, especially among cats that are given food they do not need to chew. This alone is probably responsible for more misery (in the form of mouth pain) than any other disease. It is a simple job for your vet, if necessary, to crack off the tartar deposits or thoroughly scale the teeth, dressing the raw gums underneath the tartar and tidying up the mouth. Bad teeth, as such, do not often occur but it is essential to be aware of this particular contingency and all the distress it can cause.

Although cats do not often experience eye trouble, no risks should be taken where vision is concerned, and any ailments that do occur must have prompt treatment. **Conjunctivitis** (pink-eye) is encountered in cats that 'fire-gaze' on the hearthrug, lie in draughty places or simply have irritant dust blown into the eyes. Fortunately, this condition is easily resolved, but it cannot always be differentiated from **corneal ulcers** or scars, although the latter usually occur only in one eye, frequently as a result of a cat fight when a claw may scratch the clear front covering of the eye. This can be difficult to detect without special surgery tests and requires effective and urgent treatment. Symptoms shared in common with conjunctivitis are closure of the eye(s), watering, reddening and pain. It is possible to bathe with cold tea or water on a pad of cotton wool, but inadvisable to use boracic and the like until your vet gives the go-ahead.

Cats often appear at surgery with their 'haws up', when the fine membrane at the inner corner of the eyes covers part of the front of the eye. This is not a specific disease, but may ensue from some other debilitating disease, from parasitic infestations or simply from lack of tip-top condition. The answer is, of course, to diagnose and treat the underlying cause, when the symptom will automatically rectify itself.

Another cause of trouble in cats is the common **abscess**. While this may be acquired as a result of a scratch from a rose thorn or from a cut, the most frequent cause is attack by another animal—usually a

tial to health as well as to looks. If not attended to at least once daily, the coat will mat up to the consistency of carpet felt, removal of which will entail a general anaesthetic at the surgery and probably a semi-bald cat, for it is often necessary to cut and thin fur forcibly to remove all the tufted mats.

In the process of washing their fur, cats—especially Longhaired types—tend to swallow sizeable quantities of hair. Small amounts may pass through without interruption but larger amounts collect in the stomach. While food and fluids can bypass this natural obstruction, the fur is regurgitated from time to time in the form of large sausage-like strings. This is a perfectly natural function, not to be confused with true vomiting, and, in most cases, requires no medication.

Cat claws grow continuously and are kept short by nibbling and scratching. Cutting of claws is necessary, therefore, only in old, infirm cats, or those kept exclusively indoors. Surgical removal of claws is deprecated by vets and is considered inhumane.

Skin disorders also account for a large number of cats attending veterinary surgeries. Characterized by

Below
Grooming all cats is essential and longhairs in particular need daily attention.

Below right
A cat's claws should not have to be clipped as they keep them at a comfortable length themselves by scratching. However, in old age it may be necessary to do it for them.

cat, but sometimes a rat, mouse or squirrel. The loose skin of the cat permits infection to drain from the point of injury downwards, so that the abscess is commonly found some distance from the site of the original wound, which may have healed some days beforehand. Emergency home treatment should be aimed at cleansing and applying frequent hot fomentations to the swelling. If serious, however, the abscess may have to be professionally drained and antibiotics prescribed.

Grooming, especially of Longhaired cats, is essen-

irritation to the cat or by hair loss from areas of the body, a clear diagnosis must be established before commencing treatment.

Skin disease in the cat is a vast subject and can only be touched upon here. Initially it may result from parasitic infestations—in order of frequency, **fleas, mites** and **lice**. Safe and effective insecticides will quickly rid the cat of its 'visitors' and clear up these conditions. Rather more perplexing, for the cure can be very slow, is **ringworm** or other fungal infection, which requires intense and prolonged therapy to clear the patient. Human contacts may also be at slight risk from such cases, transmission having been known between cat and owner.

Probably the commonest skin disorder, non-infectious in nature, is **military eczema**. This condition is exhibited as scab formation with hair loss down the back from neck to tail, occasionally involving head and belly. There is probably no single cause, but factors that must be eliminated are fleas, dietary imbalance, allergies, excessive or prolonged exposure to hot environments, and hormonal contributions (the disease being most frequent in neutered cats). As for treatment, new drugs have recently made a great difference, so that the condition is no longer the problem it once was.

Internal disorders

Cats of any age may suffer from two quite distinct types of worms which inhabit the bowel. **Tapeworms**, the commoner, are probably less serious and are contracted by the cat swallowing, in the course of grooming itself, a flea or louse which carries the in-

fection. Tapeworms may grow to several feet in length and can cause loss of condition, especially in the coat. They can be detected by inspection of the cat's droppings or of the fur around the anus, where segments of the 'tape' are visible, resembling grains of rice.

Roundworms may pose some threat of infection to humans and should be treated promptly. They may be passed in motions or vomited. Unlike tapeworms, they are usually present in large numbers so that when voided they resemble piles of white earthworms – 2–6 inches long – with an overall appearance of spaghetti. It is advisable to dose a cat with separate preparations, depending on the type of worm, for there is some doubt as to the effectiveness of medicines claiming to rid the cat of both types of worm in a single dose. The simplest doses are in tablet form. Follow instructions on the packet or as given by your vet; and *never* worm a sick cat, a kitten under six weeks of age, or an aged cat, without veterinary advice. While it is wise to worm a new kitten for roundworms, it is unnecessary to give regular doses unless the presence of worms is seen. Cats with tape-

Right
A beautiful healthy cat on the alert in long grass. A cat's hearing is extremely sensitive, perhaps even more so than that of a dog. Inside the ear there are semi-circular canals on which the cat depends for its balance. It is these that help the cat to right itself when it drops from a height.

worms should be examined for the presence of fleas or lice and, if detected, these should be eradicated in an effort to prevent reinfection of the worms.

Vomiting and **diarrhoea** are not infrequent complaints in the veterinary surgery. While it is obviously important for the vet to diagnose the symptoms and treat them accordingly, it would be fair to say that most may be attributed to chills of dietetic origin or to gastro-enteritis infections quite unrelated to the acute viral enteritis mentioned earlier. As a general rule, initial home treatment should be complete fasting for up to 24 hours. Small amounts of fluid–ideally boiled tap water with a little dissolved glucose–may be permitted if a thirst is apparent. The recovering patient also benefits from dietary consideration, and the best regime is to offer daily four to six small meals of light, easily digested foods, such as cooked eggs, grated cheese, and cooked fish, rabbit or chicken, depending on the cat's preference.

Kidney disease is a common cause of death in older cats. It is nowadays doubted whether the kidneys are actually infected, as was once thought, for it is more likely that death is due to sheer age degeneration of the complex tissues comprising the vital excretory organs. Possibly a malignant cancer condition accounts for a proportion of cats diagnosed as having this terminal **nephritis**. The picture is one of progressively increasing thirst, loss of weight, eventual failing appetite, tendency to vomiting (especially of food), collapse and death. Palliative treatment, if commenced early, will help to prolong life, but the end, regretfully, is inevitable; and it is much less selfish to put an ailing cat out of its misery before the distressing final stages of the illness are reached.

A particular problem, most common in neutered cats, affecting the urinary system, is the acute affliction of **urolithiasis**. This is the building-up in the bladder of fine, gravel-like particles which aggregate to form a complete blockage of the fine urethra through which urine is passed from the bladder to the exterior; this will result in total inability to pass urine and demands immediate attention and skilled veterinary treatment. The cat, often living outdoors, may not show symptoms to its owner unless its predicament is demonstrated by fruitless manoeuvres in a litter tray indoors. This condition may be linked with **cystitis** (inflammation of the bladder), and other factors, such as diet and fluid intake, are regarded as being contributory. Prompt surgical remedy is needed and strict attention should be paid to veterinary advice in order to prevent recurrence, which is always considerably more serious than the first attack.

Finally, a brief mention of four conditions almost specific to the feline species.

Viral respiratory infections are extremely common. They are airborne in droplet form and vary in type from a mild snuffle and sneeze (like the human cold) to a full, serious pneumonia, with dehydration, weakness and lack of appetite. As, at time of writing, there is no effective vaccine available against this generalized infection, speedy attention should be paid to the obvious symptoms which herald this type of disease. It is highly infectious to other cats and great importance can be placed upon home nursing, for the currently available antibiotics used by the vet will only go part-way towards resolving the infection.

Feline infectious anaemia is a slow and progressive loss of circulating red blood cells, as a result of their destruction by a microscopic parasite which may well be transmitted by biting insects such as lice and fleas. Though not thought to be highly infectious to other in-contact cats, it is a long, slow disease, and difficult to diagnose (even from blood smears which *may* show the parasite) until its severest stages have been reached. Fortunately, treatment with specific antibiotics is usually effective, but the one great problem is that the cat may be beyond hope by the time the disease is definite. Suspicious signs are scanty appetite and loss of weight over a period of weeks, visible pallor of gums, lips and eye-lining, and apparent weakness.

Feline infectious peritonitis is another fatal condition of variable course, affecting cats of all ages. It is thought to be caused by a virus and rarely, if ever, responds to treatment. It is usually an acute disease, accompanied by a high temperature and a progressive swelling of the abdomen, due to accumulation of dropsical fluid from the peritoneum which lines the abdomen and its contents. This infection may progress to a pleurisy-like chest involvement, with resultant difficulty in breathing. In the first stages the patient is obviously extremely ill and veterinary diagnosis must be sought immediately.

Lymphosarcoma is a leukaemia-like malignant or cancer condition, affecting cats of all ages, sexes and types. It is known to be caused by a virus and may be transmissible to humans, who would then display symptoms of leukaemia. In its early stages it is impossible to be certain about diagnosis, and confirmatory steps are not always easy. Initially the cat exhibits listlessness, poor appetite and possibly vomiting. Weight loss and a 'haggard' look are also typical. The disease progresses to one of three forms, one attacking the bowel, one the chest contents and one the superficial lymph nodes just underlying the skin in various parts of the body. Symptoms are of a general fast wasting and vary according to the form or site of growths. Any form of treatment to delay the disease, once diagnosed without doubt, is strongly to be condemned. Apart from increasing the risk to human contacts, the outcome of this horrible disease is invariably fatal, and mercy must be shown to the suffering cats.

While it is obviously impossible to cover many aspects of cat ailments, disease and accident in this short space, it is to be hoped that the simplified account given above of the commoner veterinary aspects may be a useful guide to all cat owners.

It is not difficult to recognize when a cat is in peak condition: the eyes, the coat, the activity and general liveliness all indicate how healthy a cat is.

Cats on Show

Grace Pond

A Tortie Colourpoint. This is a magnificent specimen and he knows it. To some people the Tortie markings are more attractive on the longhaired Colourpoint than on the shorthaired Siamese. Breeders have had problems in achieving a true dark blue eye colour.

Following page
A Blue Tortie Point Siamese kitten with a cat-nip mouse. Tortie Points come in the four Siamese colours – Seal, Blue, Chocolate and Lilac and all Torties are classified as a single separate breed at the shows. The different Siamese colours are shown in individual classes.

The history of show cats really began thousands of years ago. Short-haired cats were worshipped in Egypt at the time of the Pharaohs and were kept as pets in other parts of Africa, in India, in China and in Japan. Much later, cats with longer coats were imported from Turkey and Persia. As a result of cross-matings over the centuries, cats were eventually produced with a wide variety of coat patterns and colourings. But it was not until the first cat show was held at the Crystal Palace in 1871 that people realized how truly beautiful the animals could be. More important still was the discovery that by careful choice of adult males and females it was possible to produce kittens that were replicas of the parents.

Cat breeding became the hobby of many in high society, even including royalty, and in due course others followed suit. One well-known breeder at the end of the nineteenth century owned as many as 80 cats and travelled far and wide through the British Isles with a retinue of servants, exhibiting and, of course, taking prizes at all the cat shows.

Many visitors came from overseas to inspect the cats and to take back kittens to their own countries, and soon shows were being held in many parts of the world, organized, more or less, along the same lines as British shows.

The format and rules regarding showing have changed little over the years. Briefly, a cat must be registered with the Governing body sponsoring the show, and must have been transferred to the exhibitor, if not bred by him, several weeks prior to the show. This regulation is sometimes overlooked and can lead to disqualification if not observed. Schedules giving details of classes, judges, times of opening and closing, fees and prize monies, and general rules and regulations, are sent out many weeks before the show.

Entry forms and correct money should be sent back to the show manager well before the closing date, since, more often than not, there is insufficient space to pen all the cats eligible for entry. It is important to make sure that the details on the entry form are exactly the same as those given on the cat's registration certificate. Incorrect information may mean disqualification and forfeiture of entry forms. About a week prior to the show, the exhibitor will receive a vetting-in card and a numbered tally which, on the day, has to be attached to a piece of white tape around the cat's neck. The number on the tally is the same as that on the cat's pen.

The day previous to the show is one of feverish activity for the show manager. She has to supervise the preparation of the hall and to make sure that tabling and pens are all erected in time for the exhibits when they arrive in the morning.

At 7 o'clock on the morning of the show, all is quiet in the hall. The numbered pens, still empty, stand on the spotlessly white paper-lined tabling. Soon there are signs of activity. The officials and stewards begin to arrive, donning white overalls. So too do the veterinary surgeons, taking up positions behind the vetting-in tables, their stewards beside them with bowls of water, disinfectants and towels at the ready.

For an hour or more the exhibitors will have been queuing up outside the hall, their cats in baskets and boxes, for they are not allowed to arrive carrying the animals in their arms or on leads. At about 7.30 or 7.45 the doors open, and the vets begin the exacting task of examining each exhibit before allowing it to be penned. The whole atmosphere is very subdued, the exhibitors chatting quietly to one another, each secretly a little worried in case, for some unforeseen reason, their entry is turned down by the vet. Could a flea have been overlooked in the final grooming? Were the ears as clean as they should be? Has the journey perhaps upset the cat a little and raised its temperature? Will a small gum ulcer have appeared in a teething kitten? Will the cat that was so healthy

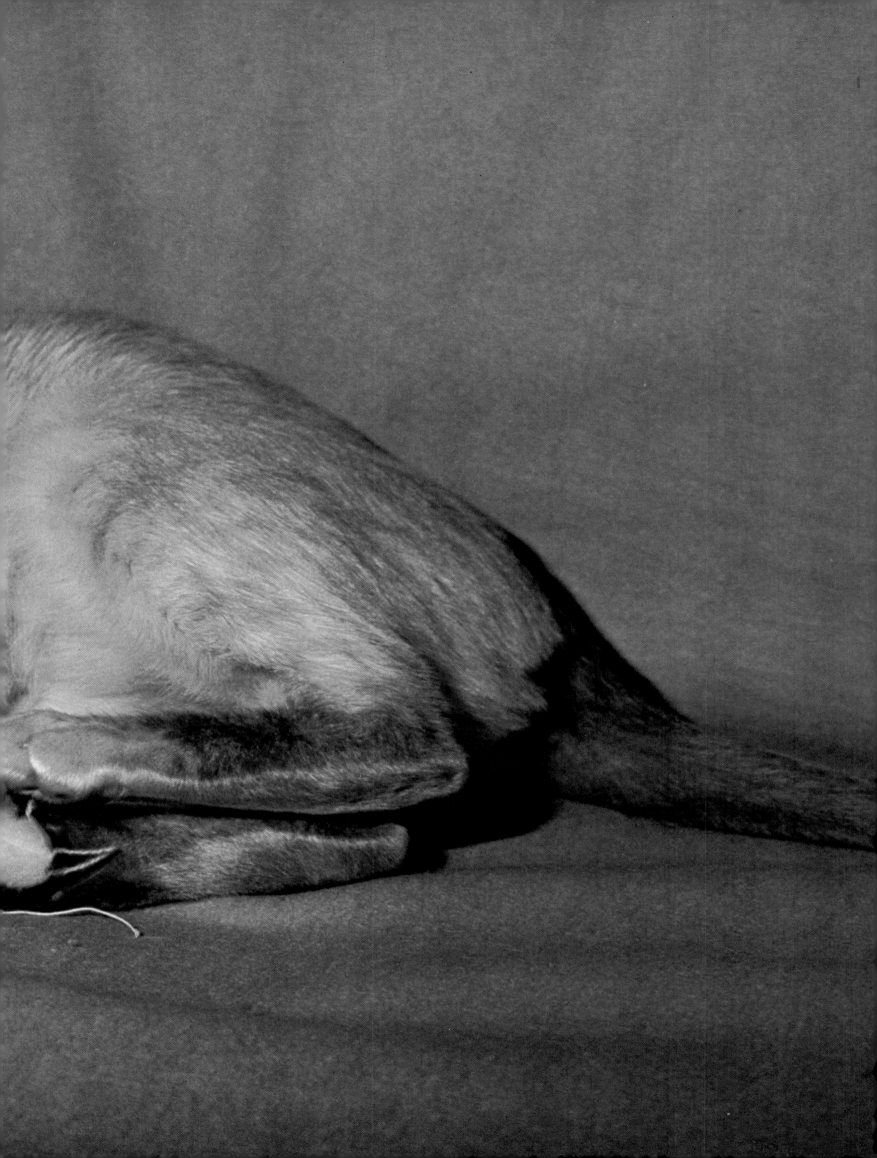

yesterday suddenly start showing signs of a cold or even a fever, thus being refused entry to the hall?

If there is the slightest doubt in the mind of the vet, he will insist on the animal being placed in an isolation pen in a separate room or—far more sensible —taken home. It may seem hard on an exhibit to be turned away for some trivial reason, but the vet not only has to consider the cat being examined but also the wellbeing of hundreds of other exhibits, any of which could pick up some infection. Most cats are now vaccinated against the potentially lethal feline infectious enteritis, but there are still other illnesses which may affect the animals, including pneumonitis, ringworm and several more.

Once the vetting-in is completed the successful exhibitors heave sighs of relief. Each cat's number is now marked off a large board and the exhibitor given a card with a large printed red 'V', to be displayed on the pen as proof that the cat has been vetted-in.

In the body of the hall, although exhibitors are now more relaxed, their main concern is to get the pen ready and to see that the cat is looking its best for the judges. There will be sufficient time later to greet old friends from last year's show and to exchange 'catty' news.

As a safeguard against infection some exhibitors wipe the wires of the pen with a piece of cotton wool dampened with a mild non-toxic disinfectant before placing the obligatory clean white blanket on the pen floor. The only other article put in the pen is a sanitary tray filled with peat (available in the hall) or, if preferred, with litter or torn-up newspaper. It does not matter if the cat decides to sleep in the tray rather than put it to proper use. No food dishes are permitted in the pens until after lunch time. It is, in fact, just as well not to feed the cat when it first arrives in the hall. It should be given time to settle down after the journey and there is a risk that, if fed, it will become sleepy and perhaps refuse to open its eyes for the judge at the vital moment.

Whether or not a cat is a good traveller, it is strictly prohibited to give it a tranquillizer before the journey. It has been found that a cat may suffer a severe reaction when the effects of such tablets wear off, becoming quite neurotic and flying at the steward and judge if they try to remove it from the pen. At one show, before this rule came into force, the public became very alarmed at the sight of what appeared to be a dead cat in a pen. Even when taken out, the animal just hung limp, apparently lifeless; but on examination by a vet, it was found to be completely tranquillized, and even when removed from the hall, took hours to revive. Any cat now found to be suffering from the effects of drugs is automatically disqualified.

As time passes, more and more owners with their cats pour into the hall. The last pens are made ready, the final grooming done. Powdering is forbidden in the hall and any powder in the coat can mean dis-

feited but, in the case of illness, provided a veterinary certificate is sent to the show manager at least a week before the show, half the fees may be returned. It is impossible to reimburse all those absent, as so much expense is involved before the show is held, including the printing of the schedule and catalogue, and the provision of a pen whether it is used or not.

In British shows, apart from the largest one in the world organized by the National Cat Club at Olympia in London, where the public are admitted throughout the day, the hall is cleared. Some halls, however, have galleries from which judging can be viewed. It is much easier for the judges to get on with their arduous unpaid task (in the United States they are paid) if there are no crowds milling around.

The majority of cats take things in their stride, sitting up in their pens surveying the scene with large, bright eyes, some obviously loving the attention they receive. The kittens, in particular, are usually very playful, showing off, dabbing at passers-by or climbing up and pulling down the numbered cards. Admittedly, there are a few who resent the whole business, turning their backs, ignoring everyone and even creeping under the blanket so that not a hair is visible. But most visitors are astonished at the good behaviour of the cats and how little noise they make.

The handling of the cat is very important. The steward has to lift the animal out of the pen and place it on the table for the judge's inspection. It must be held gently but firmly, never by the scruff of the neck. The majority make no objection to being brought out of the pen, but there is the occasional miscreant, defying with tooth and nail any attempt to handle it. Such a cat has to be passed over, otherwise the steward or judge may receive a bad bite or scratch. If a cat behaves in this way at a show, it is as well not to enter it again.

The judges start with the Open or Breed classes, in which all the cats and kittens are of the same variety. Wins in such classes are important. If the winner is an adult male, its success may be noted by the owner of a female (queen) as a future mate; if a female, she may have her name taken as a possible breeder of prize-winning kittens.

Before judging begins, any exhibitor showing two cats should make quite sure that each is in its correct pen. It has happened that two exhibits have been reversed, the mistake only being discovered after judging, which is too late, for both cats will be disqualified. A cat may, in theory, be entered for a maximum of twelve classes, but this is really excessive, for if a number of judges are involved, it will have to be taken out and put back far too many times. A novice should only put a cat in a few classes to see how it behaves.

By lunch time the Open classes should have been judged and work will have begun on the Miscellaneous and Club classes. It is at about this time that the public are admitted and the owners allowed to

qualification by the judge. It is said that at one early show an exhibitor deliberately rubbed powder into the fur of a rival black cat so that her own pet could win!

It is nowadays obligatory for each cat to be placed in a pen but nearly a century ago there were ring classes at shows, very much as at modern dog shows. This practice was ended after an occurrence at one show, for while a group of elegantly clad Edwardian ladies were marching around the ring with the gaily beribboned pets in tow, one cat made a 'savage onslaught' on another, spoiling its show chances for ever! It is recorded that a Russian princess who was there to distribute prizes preserved a remarkable equanimity 'despite the screaming of several ladies' and the severe scratching of a gentleman judge who attempted bravely to separate the cats. At the same show, apparently, when the princess tried to caress a prize-winning Chinchilla, it made a most 'savage snap' at her fingers. There is no note of her ever attending another show.

At last all the cats are vetted-in and soon after 10 o'clock the show manager calls for the hall to be cleared so that the judges can start their mammoth task of visiting each pen. Every judge is accompanied by a steward with a table on which there is a bottle of diluted disinfectant or a bowl of warm water with disinfectant, and a towel, so that the hands can be washed after each exhibit has been examined.

There may, for various reasons, be some absentees. A cat may have been turned down by the vet, have proved to be in kitten or have started calling; or an exhibitor may have been prevented by bad weather from reaching the hall. As a rule, the number of missing entries is very low. Such entry fees are for-

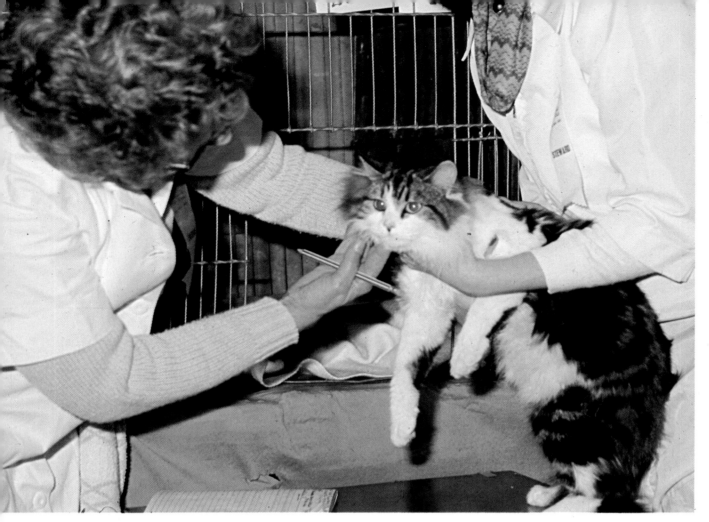

Left
Judging a Tortoiseshell entry in the Pets class of the National Cat Show at Olympia 1974. The entries are judged on their health, general well-being and well-cared for appearance.

Below
An odd-eyed white Cornish Rex cat. The curly Rex coat can be transferred to a cat of any colour and Rex cats were recognized as a listed Shorthaired breed in 1967. Rex cats are very lively, hardy and individualistic, and are rewarding cats to have at home.

Right
A Shorthaired Cream of excellent type. Well bred kittens of this breed are quite hard to come by as it is difficult to breed out the tabby markings on the face, legs and tail.

visit the pens to see their cats. If the judge is still at a pen, however, the owner should not approach while the cat is being examined. In due course slips showing the prizes awarded by the judges are put up on an award board and exhibitors flock around to see how their cats have fared. The actual prize cards start being placed on the pens shortly after lunch.

Cats are judged according to the standards set by the Governing Council of the Cat Fancy, with 100 points being allocated for the various characteristics required for what would be considered the perfect cat of a particular variety. Such an ideal cat is yet to be born, but each judge has in her mind's eye a picture of such an animal and judges each exhibit accordingly. Naturally, opinions of various judges may differ, which is as well for the exhibitor; but occasionally a cat is so outstanding and comes so close to the ideal standard that all the judges concur, and the pen becomes covered with red first prize cards, much to the admiration of passers-by.

Some shows now make awards for Best of Breed, in which the prize-winning male and female of each variety are compared with each other, the better of the two receiving a rosette and a special card.

The climax of many shows is the award for Best in Show. This is decided by separate panels of judges, one for Short-hairs, one for Long-hairs and one for Siamese – the three sections into which most shows are subdivided. Each judge nominates one cat, one kitten and one neuter to be considered by the Best in Show panel. Such nominees must have come first in their respective Open classes. The spectators crowd around the platform to watch the panels examine the cats which are brought up by the stewards. The atmosphere becomes electric as voting proceeds. Sometimes the decision is unanimous, but occasionally a referee judge is called in to give a casting vote. When a result is declared the cat is held up to be generally admired before taking a place of honour in a specially decorated Best in Show pen.

American show procedure is very different from that of the British. They have Open classes but no Miscellaneous and Club classes. The entrance system and the regulations are very similar, full details being given on a so-called premium list (equivalent to the British schedule), listing the prizes and cups which may be won. Whereas in Britain there is a separate fee for each class, in the United States there is one overall fee.

Many of the American shows are two-day events, as against a single day in Britain. The hours of judging may also be longer, closing time being 8 or 9 p.m. rather than 5.30 to 6 p.m.

The principal difference, however, is that the judging is done in rings and that a show may actually consist of four separate shows, sponsored by four clubs, with their own rings and judges, working simultaneously. The judge in one ring will not know the results in another ring, but a cat may be entered

in two, three or even four of the shows, and perhaps win in each.

In an American show the judge sits at a long table, with a row of about ten pens behind her. On entering the show, each exhibitor is told approximately at what time her cat will be judged. When her number is called, she takes the cat up and places it in the numbered pen pointed out by the ring steward. Each judge has a clerk (with similar functions to a steward in Britain) who keeps a record of the judge's points for each cat and the award given. The judge herself handles the cat, replaces it in the pen, and, where applicable, awards the appropriate ribbon. In Britain a red rosette is awarded for a first place, but in America a blue ribbon is given to the winner, a red ribbon to the second-placed cat and a yellow ribbon to the cat coming third.

In America a cat that has never previously been entered in a show is classified as a Novice; and one that has already won a prize enters the Open class. Champions are entered in the Champion class and Grand Champions in the Grand Champion class. In Britain a cat can only become a Champion by winning three Open classes at three separate shows under three different judges; and having won three Championships under similar conditions, it can enter for the Champion of Champion classes. In the United States, however, it is theoretically possible for a cat to enter as a Novice and finish up as a Champion. A winning cat will be transferred to the next class up— from Novice to Open class and, if it wins this, to the Champion class. A red, white and blue ribbon is given to the Best Cat. If the Best Cat in Show is a male,

the second-placed cat, should she be female, will be known as the BOX (Best Opposite Sex) Cat, and vice-versa.

As a rule, there are more prizes to be won in American shows than in Britain. In many shows, for example, there are special awards, rosettes and trophies, not only for the first three places but for fourth, fifth and sixth as well. Furthermore, the exhibits may also participate in a competition organized by *Cats* magazine, in which points are awarded and recorded for wins at every show. The cat scoring the most points throughout the show year is declared overall winner and receives a great deal of publicity as well as valuable prizes.

Whereas in Britain there may be as many as 60 cats or kittens of a particular variety in the Open or Breed class, all competing against one another, in the United States numbers are far fewer.

Since the American judges do not proceed to the individual pens, there is more latitude given to exhibitors who are allowed to hang coloured curtains inside the pens, choosing those which set off their cats to best advantage. Rosettes and ribbons previously won may be displayed and frequently the pens contain little beds, lace curtains and other forms of decoration. The overall effect is very festive and the public are freely admitted at all times.

Whatever the conditions and wherever the shows are held, the cats are always great attractions; and throughout the world the Cat Fancy has become virtually an international institution, with many long-lasting friendships being formed between people with a common love of cats.

Above
A Black Longhaired kitten with an excellent coat. If you have a pedigree Black Longhair and would like to show it later you will have to impose certain restrictions since the black coat can quickly go rusty coloured if the kitten spends a lot of time out of doors.

Right
The Silver Tabby is another favourite show cat because of its striking colouring. They have recently become very popular and have most attractive, shy and gentle temperaments.

Eastern Magic

Olivia Manning

Chocolate Point Siamese up a tree.

Siamese cats were rare in the seaport town where I grew up. Few people had even heard of them. My father had never forgotten two Siamese kittens he had known in the Orient a long time before. He had joined the Royal Navy in the days of sail and when very young, was sent to the Far East. Somewhere among all those places that came into his stories—Hangchow, Kowloon, Borneo, the Celebes—someone presented a pair of Siamese kittens to his ship. They were wild little creatures that chased one another up the rigging, leaping like flying foxes from rope to rope, then rushing down to roll on the deck in mock battles. When they were exhausted, they slept in each other's arms. They were the delight of the sailors.

One day the admiral's wife came on board and she, too, was amused by the kittens. She told the Captain she simply must have one of them and at once it was passed down to the leading seaman that the men were required to present—quite voluntarily, of course—a kitten to the Admiral's wife. So one kitten was taken away and the other was left to play alone. A day or two later a message came to the ship that the kitten ashore was pining for its companion and could the second kitten be sent to join it? So both kittens left the ship and the sailors could no longer watch in wonder as they leapt overhead and fought their mock battles round the deck. For all I know they fared much better in the admiral's house than they could ever have done among shipboard rough and tumble, but the story filled me with rage against authority and I felt their loss as much as did the sailors. Not that I ever did lose them for in my imagination they still play among the rigging against the flamingo and persimmon colours of a tropical sunset. And because of them I longed to have one of these kittens for my own.

Owl from the Orient

Our first Siamese kitten would sit looking at us with blue, owl-like eyes. Owl became her name but as no-

one can comfortably call 'Owl, Owl, Owl,' we called her Hibou (Siam having once been a French possession) and this became Siamesed into Eebou.

Just as there is never another baby like the first, so there is never another Siamese like the first. Every one that comes after is a sort of analogue of the original. We have had kinder and more worthy cats, but Eebou had a magic of her own. As a kitten, she was a wonder among kittens. Her successors had the disadvantage of being male. The inventiveness and engaging coquetry of Siamese kittenhood is concentrated in the female, for the female, that needs the courage of the lion and the cunning of the fox to rear her kittens in the jungle, is far more astute and inventive than the male.

Eebou was intelligent and extravagantly charming. She would claim my attention by sitting like a fur slipper on my foot. Her white breast curving over my instep, she would stare into my face with her round, unblinking, owlish eyes. When she wanted something, she demanded it with howls. Sometimes she cried for horse-meat, sometimes whale, sometimes rabbit (this was during the war). She would starve rather than eat one of these when she had a whim for another. During the time she lived with us she must have eaten her way through a dozen horses and whales, and a hundred rabbits, yet she remained a small cat, very slender and sinuous, whose poses had a ballet-dancer's flow and certainty. At night she would sometimes sleep with my husband, sometimes with me. As she crept, smooth and cool, into one's arms, she would purr so the bed seemed to quiver with her purring. When we returned after an absence from the flat, she would welcome us by flinging herself in ecstasy at our feet and would lie there, pretending to be comatose until one of us picked her up. If I came in with my arms full of parcels so I could do no more than step over her, she would hurry on in front of me and fling herself down again until I was free at last to pick her up and make a fuss of her. Then her purring became a little smug as though a

95

Left
A Seal Point Siamese running in typical Siamese fashion, maybe in fun after the end of a game or maybe in alarm, before jumping up a tree. Leaping down later rarely presents problems to a Siamese; they are particularly agile and graceful cats. If you encourage Siamese to play and retrieve their toys they will learn to chase after them again and again and amaze you with a dance of ever-increasing speed and skill.

Right
A Tabby Point Siamese also enjoying a garden. However, he seems to have little patience for a small, but brave kitten who is in his way.

tiresome situation had righted itself in a proper fashion.

There was one chair she had decided to tear to ribbons. We could only hope she would be content with it. We were furnishing at the time and when any new piece of furniture arrived, she would rush at it with outstretched claws rousing me to squeal in protest, at which she would streak off, tumbling over herself with inward laughter. Preparations for visitors put her into a frenzy of excitement so she would bolt about the rooms like a clockwork car, but when the visitors arrived she would sulk under a chair or show sudden, unreasonable jealousy that could be savage. One evening, when we were all too absorbed in conversation to notice her, she sat at my feet staring into my face then, rising with a sudden upward movement, she lunged at my eyes. Afterwards she was contrite, knowing I had had a narrow escape.

Mother and kittens

As she grew out of kittenhood, that sweet time, a new fierceness grew in her. Then a terrible thing happened: she was, as D. H. Lawrence put it, 'crucified into sex'. We were all crucified, for she howled day and night and nothing would take her mind off her frenzy.

Of course we should have had her spayed but we listened to stories of cats who lost interest in life after the operation, cats who ceased to wash themselves and cats who died, and we hoped for the alternative of Eebou transformed by the serenity of motherhood. With this vision in mind, I took her again and again to a stud-cat that lived on the outskirts of London. These journeys resulted in a phantom pregnancy that collapsed with dramatic suddenness when we moved house. At last, after heaven knows how many lovers'

meetings, Eebou produced two kittens that seemed to be dead and had to be coaxed to life on a hot-water bottle.

Eebou in the part of devoted mother, becoming more anxious as the kittens became more adventurous, was a delightful interlude that had been reached by such an ordeal of uproar, uncertainty—slow trains to the suburbs, delivering her one day, returning for her the next—of failure, of starting again, to say nothing of the cost, that it was scarcely possible to contemplate a repeat performance.

Meanwhile there were the kittens and the exquisite respite of Eebou's absorption in them. She hid them to begin with in the lowest drawer of a chest of drawers. As soon as they were old enough to climb out, she begged for the drawer just above to be opened and carried them up there, a journey for each, and purred with content when they were again under her paw. In a day or two they would find their way down from the second drawer and have to be carried up to the next. Soon there was no height they could not negotiate and as they swung down from drawer to drawer in the first wonder of independent existence, Eebou watched, and gave little mews of concern and looked at us, pleading with us to restrain them. She was so absorbed in her anxious happiness, how could we ever deprive her of this natural condition?

As soon as they began to develop, the kittens became known as the Big Kitten and the Little Kitten. Both were males. We had to sell one of them and the young man who came to look at them at once chose the Big Kitten.

The Little Kitten was such a pathetic scrap of a thing we decided there was nothing to do but keep him. We named our kitten Faro after the cat in a novel which I published about that time. The fictional cat was a portrait of Eebou and a female, but Faro accepted the name without complaint.

The kittens were no age at all when Eebou started calling again. Her high penetrating cry that scarcely stopped day and night had got us into trouble the first time it started up. In Bloomsbury she had sat in the window and screamed so appealingly at the passers-by that people put notes in the letter-box accusing us of leaving her locked up alone to starve. One woman offered to give us advice on the care of Siamese cats, saying she had had two, one of which died by jumping out of a window and the other had pined and died while she was staying with her father. So we had not only to suffer Eebou's ceaseless cries but somehow to keep them hidden from the neighbourhood.

In the new flat matters were worse. The man who had an office below us did not care if Eebou were locked up or starving, but he was furious about the noise she made. He complained to the landlord. We were warned.

Things could not go on as they were. Apart from the complaints, the sleepless nights were telling on us.

We decided at last she must go to the country and return to us when we found a flat or a house where a cat could have freedom and call to her heart's content.

Here the story grows sad and tragedy enters. Eebou's two-kitten-triumph produced in her a feverish desire for more and more kittens. Production-line quantity, rather than quality, became her aim, so she would break out from any stronghold and entice to her purposes the shabbiest toms. She did not take to the rigours of country life. She would sneak into the homes of rich neighbours, seeking comfortable solitude away from the other cats and dogs among which she now lived, and curl up on silken counterpanes. Her new guardians thought her a selfish, moody, difficult cat but, unfortunately, kept this opinion to themselves and politely pretended they were pleased to have her. Then one day they gave her away to a kindly woman who knew nothing of the habits of the female Siamese and was shocked when she gave forth her uproarious jungle call. At last I discovered that Eebou had changed her home and was unwanted everywhere; I asked that she might be returned to me. She had with all her faults, a beauty, a quality of magic which makes lovable so many selfish and difficult creatures, humans as well as cats.

It was arranged. She was to return to us, but, alas, we never saw her again. It was sex that finished our poor Eebou. A few days before her arranged departure, she broke out of the house and took her last ride on the non-stop streetcar named 'Desire'. She was, perhaps, like so many modern heroines, a doomed creature from the start.

Crossing a main road in darkness, she was struck by a car. We can only hope she was killed at once. By morning nothing remained of her beauty. The flow and certainty of her movements were lost for ever.

Faro—a study in contentment

Faro was a problem kitten from the beginning. He had been a victim of his brother, Big Kitten, who was now christened Butch. Butch had grown twice as fast as Faro and had soon become a fat bully who badgered his little brother unmercifully. There was enough milk for both of them but Butch believed it was all meant for Butch alone. Whenever Faro settled down for a feed, he was pushed aside by his dreadful brother and as a result, developed an enduring sense of deprivation and the hardness of life.

Despite his magnificence, Butch did not last long. His new home was a flat and like all pent-up cats, he was curious about the world outside. One day, when by accident flat door and street door were open together, he made a bolt for it and met his death beneath the wheels of a passing taxi. Faro was to outlive him for twelve years or more.

Once the overwhelming figure of Big Kitten left his life, Faro started to grow and when he reached maturity, he was the classical Siamese, of normal size and strongly shaped like his champion sire. Except for his pale eyes, he seemed to have inherited nothing

from his sleekly elegant little mother. He had none of her vitality or the sense of delight in life that made her death all the more painful to us. We remembered her as an Ariel, all caprice and sweetness, and forgot how our adored little friend had changed into a fiend, impatient of us and everything else that had once made her world.

As for Faro, he went early to the vet, and if he were deprived of the excitements of sex he was also saved from its miseries.

Faro developed into a comfortable teddy-bear cat. Though he lacked Eebou's grace and sparkle, he had unusual strength of character. What he wanted, he had to have. There could be no compromise. He would not let the matter drop. Humour was not his strong point. There had been times when Eebou seemed to be rolling about with laughter, but the most to be expected from Faro was a murmur of contentment when all was well. I soon learnt not to make fun of him. Once or twice when he was disgruntled because of the weather or some other hardship beyond my influence, I bent over him, commiserating in a suspect tone, and received a belt with a paw that soon put an end to that

sort of joke. Although poor Butch had gone so early to the Elysian fields, his shadow overhung Faro's life. Otherwise it was not an eventful life. Faro was a good cat, a devoted cat, but like an old bachelor of indefectible behaviour, he expected the world about him to be indefectible, too. Its shortcomings made him peevish and he had often to be cosseted back to good humour. His chief needs were warmth and comfort; not, as one might suppose in view of his infantile trauma, food. He was very difficult to feed. Those who imagine that any cat will eat if it is hungry, have never experienced the obstinacy of a fastidious Siamese. The owner is at a disadvantage not only because he loves the creature but because he hates to see so much good food go to waste.

'You spoil that cat,' said the butcher, a fat jolly fellow who was known to keep the best cuts for himself: 'Give 'im lights–'e'll eat 'em if 'e 'as to. Starve 'im till 'e does eat 'em, that's my advice.'

At first I was not greatly interested in Faro, accepting him as Eebou's son but seeing him a more sedate and less engaging creature. He was also something of a problem for we were moving to a St John's

101

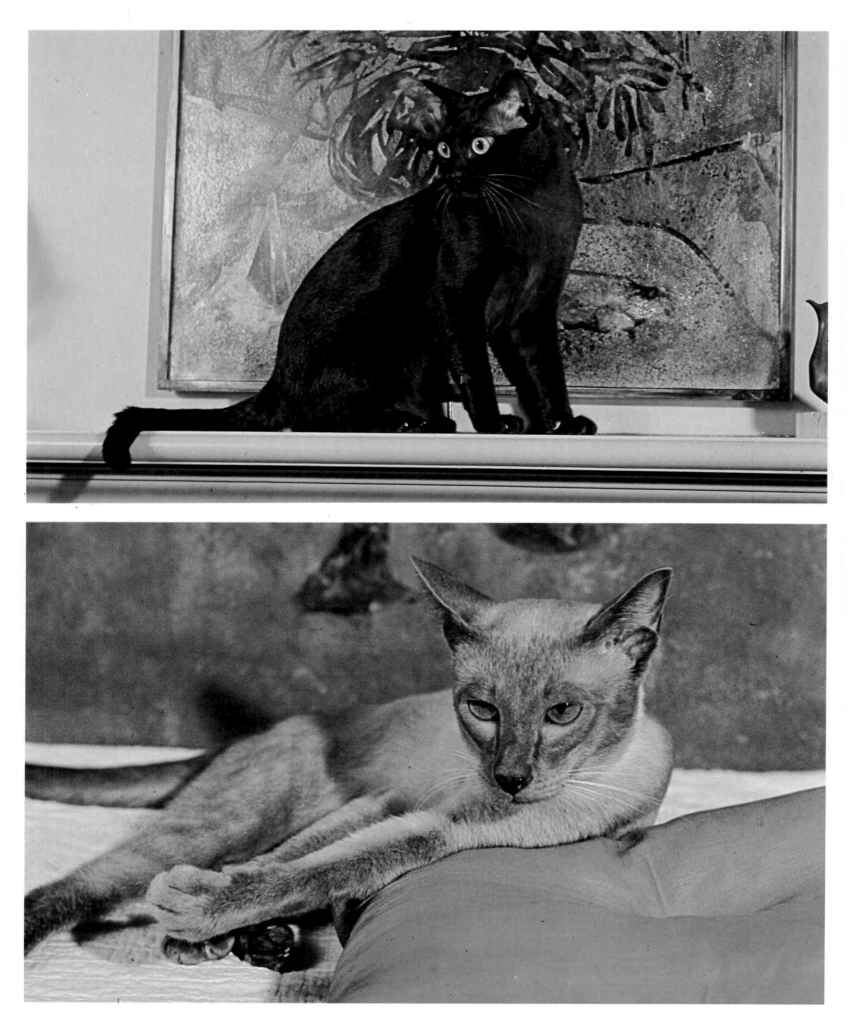

Wood house and we had arranged to be abroad for a month before the move. He had to stay with my mother for two months and she was not enthusiastic about such long responsibility for someone else's pet. On our return to England, with the move hanging over us, I paid my mother a weekend visit. Faro was sitting in the hall. I picked him up. Purring, he passed his cold, small nose over my face then gave several crowing cries of joy, more intense and intimate than the welcoming barks of a dog. When I put him on the floor he rushed up and down stairs in a fury of rejoicing, loosening stair-rods and scattering rugs.

'He knew you were coming back,' my mother said. 'He would not go into the garden. He sat all day in the hall watching the front door.'

How did he know that I was coming? My mother's bustling expectation may have alerted him—yet to argue from it that someone was expected, and the person must be I, called for no small reasoning power. It is easier to see it as a case of thought transference.

Faro, though lacking his mother's insouciant charm and flights of fancy, had the confidence of belief in his own virtue. He led a quiet life. I can only twice remember his getting into a fight so furious that he came back torn and slept for hours, exhausted. He was not really a fighter. My Burmese, Miou, goes out looking for trouble but Faro was too near the human avatar for that. One tended to think of him as a human being—a gentle good-tempered old boy, not assertive

but, at the same time, not lacking in quiet self-esteem.

The Blue Point and the Burmese

After Faro died we adopted a Blue Point Siamese named Choula. He was a staid cat, lazy and greedy, and it must have seemed that in possession of an untroubled home where meals were regular and plentiful, he had nothing more to worry about. We thought so, too. We could not have imagined that by giving him a charming, loving little companion we would break his heart.

I was offered a Brown Burmese kitten which I found impossible to refuse. Choula had been with us so short a time, we supposed he would accept another cat as part of the established order of things. He did nothing of the sort. When I brought the little creature in, he stared at it, aghast.

The kitten, whose registered name was Ngo Ah-Miou, was a creature of delectable prettiness. His silken coat was the colour of snuff; he had a seal-dark line down his spine and a seal-dark mask; his eyes were topaz. He was most lovable and because we loved him so much ourselves, we were sure that very soon Choula would love him, too. We were wrong.

On the first day, as the kitten explored the house, Choula stalked it, keeping at a safe distance, occasionally sitting down, the better to observe its every movement. He seemed possessed by an intent interest, but not more than interest. He may have seen the

A Brown Burmese and Blue Point Siamese. Cats often seem to demonstrate that they have an aesthetic sense – they choose to sit and pose in places which match their colouring. Blue to match blue eyes, orange flowers to match a marmalade cat, white to offset rich burnished brown. And cats dance, and listen to music – sometimes – and can sit for hours, their ears twitching at sounds and sights unperceived by humans.

kitten as merely a temporary intruder, like a bird or a mouse. But in the evening, when we were sitting by the fire, Choula, on my knee, stared down at Miou playing on the hearthrug and seemed to realize that the kitten had come to stay. Suddenly, he gave a long drawn cry, agonized and angry. I put my hands on him to soothe him and felt his body tremble. He gave another cry, then another and another. These hoarse cries seemed to come from his very bowels.

Miou stopped and watched Choula, surprised but not alarmed by the terrible noise. Having just come from his mother, he was used to the presence of a large, furry protector; he seemed to see Choula as a similar, perhaps even identical, figure. As one cry followed another, Miou sat alert, delighted by the uproar.

What were we to do? We loved both cats and could only hope they would learn to live together. The problem was made more difficult by Miou's deep affection for Choula. Whenever he tired of playing Miou would nestle against Choula and lick him to show friendliness. Choula, unnerved, would shy away, leaving Miou bewildered by the rebuff.

Miou's vitality was a source of wonder and horror to Choula. Eebou had been vivacious enough but Miou was frenzied. He had the ability to rise directly from the ground. If in his play, he came upon some unexpected trifle—a button, a pea-pod, a feather—he would fly up to a height of four or five feet and seem to pause there in astonishment.

Left
A full-grown healthy Brown Burmese with a gleaming, shiny coat.

Below
A young Burmese kitten showing the fluffy lighter coat that will later develop into the sleek and darker fur of the adult cat.

Miou the mischief-maker

The Burmese is the wildest of all kittens, climbing anything that can be climbed with a flash-speed that defeats the eye. Miou was not only likely to be 'surprised by joy' but life so elated him that he spent all his waking hours tearing up and down curtains, springing on to shelves and cupboard tops, and taking whole flights of stairs at a bound. Watching in dismay, Choula obviously regarded the whole exhibition as deplorable.

One day Miou found he could unroll the lavatory paper. Standing upright and spinning the roll with his paws, he would get a heap of paper around him, then cavort about in it, bringing down more and more paper, until the whole roll would be on the floor in ribbons. When we began to put the rolls out of reach, he looked for new entertainment and found a pound packet of cotton wool. I returned home to find the bathroom floor white with the torn-up cotton wool and Miou rampaging about in it like a little dark fiend. Choula, safe on the top of the clothes basket, gazed with the incredulous hostility of middle-age scandalized by the antics of lawless youth. He turned his head when I entered and looked at me as though to ask, 'How long can this go on?'

Not long. The cat's entrancing infancy is brief. Time subdued Miou's ebullience and slowly restored Choula to peace of mind. Though he would not tolerate Miou on the bed, he began to tolerate him as a sleeping companion on the sofa or before the fire. This intimacy

A Blue Burmese, a Red Point Siamese, a Blue Point Siamese and two Brown Burmese kittens.

established, Choula submitted to be licked and one day began to lick back. This began the game of licking and counterlicking: two tongues travelling busily from coat to coat, so neither cat knew whether he licked his neighbour or himself. The game, that usually began after meals, was partly social and partly practical, for a good hunter must be odourless. When, as sometimes happened, Choula did not want to be licked, he would lick back in urgent protest, his gaze raised, intent and pleading, too polite or too nervous to stop Miou with a blow. At other times, asserting himself as though taking action against his own timidity, Choula would pin Miou down and wash his face with determined thoroughness, Miou submitting like a kitten beneath its mother's paw.

As Miou matured, his coat darkened. His belly fur kept its rich snuff brown but the rest took on the colour, as well as the lustre, of the darkest mink. One evening as he ran past us on the stairs, a visitor asked: 'Why is that cat more black than other black cats?'

'Because he is brown,' I said.

Miou undoubtedly is an 'all over seal' cat. In sunlight the maroon of his fur has the glint of copper. He is not only the colour of those sealskin coats our grandmothers wore, he has the same texture. I have never known a cat with such delicate fur. He is now so dark that he can easily hide in the shadows beneath sofa or bed, but his eyes, of topaz gold, give him away as they gaze out with the fearless innocence of one who has always been loved.

His dark paws have the feel of velvet, his touch the delicacy of a feather. In the morning, wanting to get the day started, he gives my face a brush with the fur round his pads. I refuse to wake – he brushes me again. And again. Each time it is the merest breath of a touch, yet it is more effective than an earthquake. I despair. I sit up. At once he flirts away, delighted by the promise of breakfast and the excitements of out-of-doors.

By now the reader may be saying, 'This is ridiculous. She writes of cats as though they were humans.' But are they so very different? The fact is that when an animal, any animal, enters one's home, it becomes something more than an animal. The change is brought about not merely by human fantasy and human need: the animal itself is drawn out of its animal world and advances to meet our wider understanding. In this way, Oriental cats, more sensitive and imaginative than other animals, come very close to those who love them. It is easy to accept the Hindu belief that they have souls and are now very near the human avatar. If this is so, we may hope that our love advances their development.

When they die – and even in these days they leave us all too soon – they live on in the mind, as individual as any human friend. That may be their only immortality, but who can tell? If we survive death, and no-one can say for sure we do not, would we not have them with us? Eebou, Faro, Choula, Miou – without their company, I would find Paradise so much the less.

Stars of Television and Film

Gladys Hayward

How often, when watching your pet cat stretching comfortably in front of the fire, kicking a ball across the floor or pretending to be a tiger in the garden, you must have wished you had a camera at the ready to record the precious moment. If only you could capture all those changing moods—the characteristic expressions and actions which tell you quite clearly whether your cat is contented or angry or amused or just plain bored. What a natural actor the cat seems to be, but when it comes to the point—as any professional photographer will confirm—what a difficult subject it really is!

One of the most appealing things about a cat is that it will never do what *you* want, unless that action happens to suit its inclinations at that particular moment. You can't just pop it down on a cushion, ask it to look at the camera and click the shutter. In the case of, say, a child, it takes two—the subject and the photographer—to make a good picture. Where the cat is concerned, it takes three. Even the most skilled photographer can do little with an unco-operative subject. If the cat refuses to take part in the 'game', he might just as well give up. This is where the third member of the trio—the trainer or handler—comes in.

Delightful cats and kittens nowadays peer out from cards, calendars, chocolate box lids, magazine covers, newspaper pages and book jackets. They pose for television commercials and they appear in films with famous actors. Most of these so-called 'working' cats are especially trained for such a career. Breeding and training them is a full-time occupation and, like any job, it has its rewards, its occasional setbacks and its peculiar problems.

The making of a star

A future feline star can often be discovered when still a kitten. Beauty is, of course, important, but most cats fulfil that simple requirement. The crucial test of

a working cat is that it should be gentle, loving and tractable. It must be placid in temperament, display no sign of nerves, show complete trust in strangers and adapt to all manner of unusual circumstances. Because cats are such individualists few will combine all these qualities, so that potential stars are not born every day. Many cats, for example, may be ideal as far as colour and temperament are concerned, but still fail to pass the vital test of immunity to studio light, noise and bustle.

Selecting a star-to-be from a litter of kittens is largely a matter of observation and experience. Our method is to let them run freely about the garden and then entice them with titbits. If one of them responds to the call every time, whereas the others saunter up only now and then, this will be the one on which it is worth concentrating.

A kitten embarking on an acting career will probably begin with 'stills' for birthday cards, calendars and so forth. Although this is a matter of simple posing rather than performing, the kitten will gain valuable experience from the travelling involved and from the movements, sounds and flashing lights that make up the studio atmosphere. By the time it has done two or three sessions of photography it will have learned that posing for the camera can be great fun.

Having persuaded it to pose for a 'still', the next stage is what is known as an 'easy' shot, in which the cat plays a passive part in a scene. This will probably involve being held by an actor or actress, which gets it accustomed to remaining quiet and still when other people are performing.

Tricks of the trade

Even training a cat to this level requires long hours of patient love and care; but the real fun (and the headaches) begin when it is ready to progress further and launch out on an acting career in its own right. Basically this is a question of getting the cat used to

Far left
Two Silver Tabbies posing perfectly for their picture.

Left
The well-trained Chinchilla who advertises carpets.

Right
Cats are natural actors and this Longhaired Silver Tabby is posing arrogantly in a chair which matches his colour. The beautiful cat below is also posing but he is dignified and aloof, pretending to be unaware of the camera's existence.

special and varied situations. Total obedience is naturally the main objective, but this can only be achieved by patience and kindness. The voice must never be raised in anger—calmness and tolerance are the golden rules. With a cat that enters into the spirit of the thing and takes positive pleasure in being trained, persistence and gentle encouragement will work wonders.

Sometimes a good deal of ingenuity on the handler's part may be entailed in order to attract the cat's attention, such as displaying toys, rattling keys and even lying flat on the floor, pretending to be another animal. Bribery, in the form of food, is essential to all training procedures. Offering a cat its favourite food is an obvious way of calling it, and this is an important part of any lesson. Getting it to sit or stand in a certain spot is basic training. This can be done by enticing it with a plate of food and encouraging it, by means of petting and talking, to stay still at the exact point you want. After a time the cat will get the spot fixed in its mind and stay put even when you remove the food, but you must, of course, reward its obedience with a titbit.

This is the way we train the beautiful Chinchillas that are required to pose on carpets for a well-known television advertisement. Once the cat has been persuaded to settle down in the right place, it is simply a matter of chatting softly and stroking her continuously, then gradually moving away. The whole procedure generally has to be repeated many times before she realizes what she is expected to do.

Confidence is all-important and the cat must have a familiar face around and, if possible, an easy bolt-hole. Provided it feels happy and contented, it will stay in one place for a lengthy period – as one of our pupils did with Peter Sellers in *The Wrong Box.*

For one advertisement a cat was required that was able to pick out the correct bowl of food—say the middle one of three—and for this we trained a tabby named Tib. After a few experimental tastes in each bowl Tib never made a mistake, and would go through the routine for the benefit of the camera time and time again. But having had enough, he would retire to his basket for a rest – a sign to the studio staff that the moment had come for their coffee break. Ten minutes later they would all begin again.

Training a cat to jump down from a high place to a given spot is also done by tempting it with food. The cat will be set on a ladder and a dish put on a table below. Gradually the distance between ladder and table is increased, and after several lessons the cat will be jumping freely from a height of six feet or thereabouts. Tib, although a large cat, specialized in high-jumping and did so in a number of films, as well as in the television series *Z Cars.*

Teaching a cat to leap through a window is not nearly so easy, its general attitude being 'Show me what's on the other side first'. The handler can usually get results by showing a plate of food or a toy through the open window and then lowering it out of camera range. Hopefully, the cat's natural curiosity will get the better of its common sense!

Ins and outs of acting
As every owner knows, a household cat can only be trained up to a certain point, and its cleverness is

limited to actions that come naturally and in which it takes pleasure. As a rule, a working cat is not expected to perform tricks, but it may have to put on fancy dress for a particular advertisement or film sequence. A cat can be trained to wear a collar, a necklace, a tiara or even a hat, and still look cool and dignified.

Incidentally, studio training is not simply confined to the central character, the cat. A recipe for a disastrous day's work is an impatient director, an actress in flimsy clothing who hates cats, grabs your pet clumsily and complains that she has been scratched, and perhaps a small child who finds the cat too heavy to carry. Surprisingly few people know how to lift and handle a cat correctly. If the star is unaware of the proper way of picking it up and caressing it, this must be explained beforehand. Needless to say, the director's attitude is also important, and if he is patient and helpful, all will go well.

Some television commercials and films call for outdoor work and this is far more complicated than ordinary studio routine. It is not easy to find a cat that will work out of doors at any time, especially one that responds to the call and does not wander off the set between takes. This needs a great deal of patience on the handler's part because any shouting (and there is usually plenty of that) is liable to send a cat scampering off. A good method of training a cat to work outdoors is to simulate a film set in some open space, preferably close to a busy road with traffic. We are lucky to have a suitable field behind our home where we spend weeks on end, if need be, getting our cats accustomed to such conditions.

One of our successful outdoor actors was Bimbo,

Below
Chinchilla queen and kittens.

a Shorthaired Black, seen in a television film *Superstitions*. He was seen wandering freely through the streets of London—secure in the knowledge that just out of camera range was his basket, to which he could soon retire. Two of our Siamese, a Seal Point named Kye and a Lilac Point called Tuptin, were also trained to work outdoors in *Endless Night* with Hayley Mills. But perhaps our greatest triumph was in *Doctor Dolittle*, in which one of our cats was trained to jump onto Rex Harrison's shoulder and feed from his hand.

Stars and stand-ins

It is normal for a leading star to have one or more stand-ins, and this is true even for a working cat. Long studio sessions under hot lights can be extremely exhausting and it is important for the star not to look tired from overwork. Posing while lighting and camera focus are adjusted, or even racing across stage in long-shot, can be done just as easily by substituting another cat of the same size, colour and temperament. In this way work can proceed without interruption and when the moment arrives for the real rehearsal and takes, the star will appear fresh and fully rested.

The most difficult film sequences featuring a number of our cats were in *Diamonds Are Forever*, the James Bond thriller. The most demanding test of our star, a Chinchilla named Clarissa, was to walk down a broad staircase which had no back or sides. After hours of training we managed to get her three-quarters of the way down, but at that point she insisted on jumping through the back of the stairs to the ground. So we had to station one handler behind the stairs with a bowl of food that she disliked intensely, and another handler at the foot of the stairs carrying a dish of her favourite food. After two or three takes she gave a perfect performance.

Our problems for this film were not yet over, for other sequences required the same white cat to have a revolver fired close to her ear. No amount of training would have persuaded Clarissa to sit quietly while this went on. So we brought in one of her stand-ins, a Blue-eyed White Persian. Being stone deaf, like most cats of this type, she did not bat a whisker during the 'shooting', and all was well.

The climax of a working cat's career may come when, as a recognized star, it is exhibited at the National Cat Club Show at Olympia, reclining in a pen designed as a miniature film set or replica of a television advertisement, basking in the admiration of the crowds. But this glory and glamour are reserved only for a chosen few. Those that do not make the grade simply go back to being ordinary cats, unemployment being no great tragedy in the feline world.

For those of us who train cats for film and television work there are pleasures and rewards, to be sure, but do remember, if you are tempted to try it, that there can be no half measures. Love, patience, skill and dedication all amount to a life's work.

The Mind of the Cat

Angela Sayer

The cat has played a prominent role on the stage of human history. Apart from being cherished as a pet and companion, it has been worshipped as a deity and persecuted as an ally of the devil. Poets, painters and sculptors have paid it honour. It has posed for photographers, starred in films and romped through the pages of fiction, legend and fairy-tale. Quite a tribute, all in all, to an animal with a most singular personality.

What is the reason for man's preoccupation through the ages with this enigmatic little creature? Could it be that he sees something of his own nature mirrored in the moods of his pet? As a species, high on the evolutionary ladder, the cat has amply proved its capacity to adapt successfully to any environment; and this has ensured it of a place in man's affections all over the world.

It is, of course, a mistake to talk of owning a cat; rather the cat consents to live with, and be fed by, its human slave. You cannot punish a cat and get away with it, for the cat will neither forget nor forgive; nor can you force a cat to do anything it has decided not to do, at risk of receiving painful proof of its strength, quite out of proportion to its size!

Maternal devotion

The domestic cat is indeed a formidable adversary, and a mother will nurture and defend her young even at the expense of her own life. A pregnant cat, searching for a suitable nesting niche, was once inadvertently imprisoned in a crate containing engine parts which was subsequently loaded into the hold of a freighter for a long sea voyage. When the crate was broken open at its destination some six weeks later, the little female was discovered in an emaciated condition, but still alive, with two kittens that were blooming and bouncing with health. Evidently she had provided milk for them by licking the protective grease from the machinery in which she was en-tombed, depleting her own body reserves to the point of near-death. Happily, with loving care from a stevedore's family, she eventually made a complete recovery.

There are many stories of mother cats which have fought to the death against marauders trying to rob them of their kittens. Dogs and feral toms will occasionally attempt to destroy young kittens, and distraught owners have returned home to find the mutilated, dying mother still overlying the babies that she has battled so fiercely to save. Owners of show dogs have had seasonal prospects ruined by allowing their exhibit access to a cat's nest box, the raking claws of an irate little queen having temporarily scarred the inquisitive snout.

A mother cat often has the urge to move her litter to another nest when they are about three to four weeks old. The interesting point about such behaviour is that this is just about the time when the nest or burrow of a wild cat would begin to be soiled by the young kittens. Although the nest box in the home is kept fresh and clean, with newly washed blankets or paper, the cat evidently feels an instinctive need to carry the members of her little family, one by one, to a new abode.

I once had a Lilac Point Siamese queen who always moved her family from the comfort of the warm kitchen to the large, airy bedroom in the attic. Her fourth litter attained the age of four weeks while the attic staircase was being renovated and so blocked off. That did not deter Laretta, however, and when we found the kitchen maternity box empty we started a long search for the missing litter, disregarding the attic, to which access was closed. After a fruitless afternoon, we removed the barricade from the attic stairs and climbed up. To our astonishment, the five little babes were asleep on the bed, but there was no sign of Laretta. We called repeatedly and at last she appeared at the open attic window, thus giving away

Left
One eye always open —
cats very rarely go to
sleep, or so it seems to us.

Right
A family that has been
disturbed; the mother is
trying to keep all her
kittens in their basket
and this is usual
behaviour on the part of
the queen who seems to
consider her kittens
should stay put for
longer than they want to.
This Tortoiseshell is
meeting with strong
defiance from one kitten.
Although the queen
picks the kittens up by
the scruff of their
neck it is not a good idea
for us to do since it is
possible to cause an
injury, particularly as
they grow older.

her secret. She had carried her kittens, one by one, through the house and up the main staircase, along the hall and out of the landing window, across a sloping roof to the dormer window, and finally into her selected place of refuge!

Early lessons

A mother teaches her kittens to eat solid foods, to play, to fight and to hunt. If she is given a mouse-sized piece of meat, she will proudly take it to her litter, put it down in front of them and give a short, sharp 'prrrp', which encourages the youngsters to emerge from the box to investigate the 'kill'. They may even lick or taste the meat, although not old enough to chew it. Then the queen will pat the morsel, so that it skitters a few inches across the floor. The babies' eyes follow it with interest and some of the bolder ones will perhaps toddle after the meat and place a possessive paw on it.

As the kittens grow, the queen will flash her tail from side to side, prompting the youngsters to pounce on 'prey'. She sets the example by tossing small pieces of meat or balls of paper into the air and then diving upon them as they land, 'prrrping' to the kittens all the while, until they follow suit. When she feels they should be weaned, she will settle down, concealing all her teats and not adopting the characteristic nursing pose which enables them to suckle. If they nuzzle and push at her, trying to nurse, she will eventually jump up onto a chair or shelf, well out of their reach.

Purring, weaving, rubbing and kneading are all signs of contentment and relaxation. The kitten begins to purr while still suckling, the sound being continuous as it breathes in and out, stopping momentarily as the milk is swallowed. As the cat grows, purring is retained as a friendly, contact-establishing sound and is often accompanied by the kneading movements of the front paws which the young kitten adopts while nursing.

The domestic cat frequently rubs lips and body against human legs, and weaves past in such a way that the tail comes in contact with the side of a table or the legs of a chair. In performing these commonplace actions the cat is, in fact, marking its territory in a very subtle way. A number of scent glands are present on various parts of the cat's body, and although such scents cannot be detected by the human nose they provide identification signals for other cats. When the cat rubs and weaves, it deposits odours from the glands on all points of contact, serving to warn off strange cats in the area. It is interesting to see how the cat rubs and weaves possessively around its owner's legs, especially when food is being prepared.

A friend's cat, renowned for these habits, decided to claim ownership to a new electric fire by rubbing his lips and flanks along the teak surround. As he turned to repeat the procedure, his tail tip flicked between the safety bars and immediately ignited, causing him to flee from the room, tail ablaze. Fortunately he was quickly wrapped in a towel and the

only injury was to his pride in sporting a blackened, brush-like appendage where his beautiful fluffy tail had been. He spat and growled at the fire for several weeks, until his new hair grew through, and never again tried to put his mark in that vicinity.

Territorial sense
Entire male cats have the habit of marking out their territory distinctly by spraying urine against any conspicuous object encountered in a daily constitutional stroll. The scent of the urine is most distasteful to humans and it is for this reason that the majority of pet males are neutered. The operation effectively removes the odour from the urine and decreases the need for the cat to spray when marking its possessions. Pedigree males, having once marked the outdoor accommodation in which they are confined (usually a large, heated hut with an attached, wired-in run) will stop spraying until visitors arrive. Many a stud owner has been embarrassed or amused, depending on his

nature, when a beloved male has abruptly turned its back on a visitor, lifted its tail and directed a well-aimed jet at knee level.

A cat investigating the scent trail left by another cat will exhibit a strange and very noticeable reaction. Its eyes half close, its mouth opens and it raises its head as if carefully savouring the scent. This, in fact, is literally what is happening. Such behaviour is known as the flehmen reaction and allows the scent to be drawn up to a special olfactory organ in the upper palate. The organ connects with a part of the brain which flashes back the vital information as to whether this particular scent has been experienced previously, and whether it has been left by friend or enemy.

Contrasts in play
Playing is a pastime that brings pleasure both to cat and owner; but different breeds seem to have their individual preferences for certain types of game. Longhaired cats have a particular fondness for

Cats and kittens spend a great deal of time washing and cleaning themselves. The first lesson kittens learn from their mother is how to wash and how to do it thoroughly. They also enjoy washing each other and deliberately choose places where they can never reach to wash themselves. A cat's tongue is rough and suited to going to the roots of even a long coat, and sometimes the cat is quite wet after a long and concentrated washing session.

squeezing into small boxes, usually a size smaller than would comfortably fit their ample frames. They also love to sit on chairs pushed snugly under the table, and to crawl into any object that is rolled up, such as a carpet or a length of linoleum. British Shorthairs derive special enjoyment from playing with pingpong balls and shuttlecocks, becoming adept dribblers and batsmen. They also love playing a game which the owner has to initiate by covering them gently with a large open sheet of newspaper. Then, with body crouched, they will dash from side to side, creating draughts that lift the paper up and bring it floating down again. Only a paw or tail tip shows from time to time as the paper flutters and bounces around the room.

Siamese cats clearly prefer some human participation in their games. One favourite pastime is to lie on their back and allow themselves to be propelled across the floor. A slippery linoleum surface is ideal for this game, for having slithered across to the other side of

There is very little kittens and cats do not know about charming their owners; by one means or another they end up having their own way.

the room, they will tear back to the starting point and demand another go. The Foreign breeds also enjoy playing with a large paper bag which has a small tear in one corner. When the edges of the bag are pushed together so that the back is held open, and it is placed on the floor, the cat will fling itself from the opposite side of the room headlong into the bag, attempting to leap through the slit at the end. The pointed nose sticks fast and there will be several minutes of rolling and cavorting before the cat reduces the bag to shreds.

Most cats love pipe-cleaner 'spiders', made by twisting together four pipe-cleaners and securing them with a piece of wool. In order to avoid scratching the cat's eyes, the end of the 'feet' should be turned back and then the 'legs' can be bent into a hooked shape so as to give a chillingly realistic appearance. I have known Siamese cats to keep such a plaything for years, taking it to bed each night and away on holiday to the boarding cattery.

One of my early Siamese, Rosie, had a series of spiders and would play at retrieving them until we were exhausted. She would give us a short recovery period, then thrust the soggy object into the nearest palm and wait expectantly for it to be thrown, preferably onto a bookshelf or behind the settee so that she could spend some time searching before pouncing for the kill. Alternatively, we would hide the spider under a rug or behind a cushion while she was out of the room. It was fascinating to watch her methodical search, using sight and smell, until she found her favourite toy.

Once, when Rosie was very ill, not having eaten of her own free will for several weeks, the vet told us that there was nothing more he could do for her. Desolate, we carried her around the garden, trying to arouse her interest in life and persuade her to fight back, but to no avail. As I sat nursing her in a shawl beside the fire, I absentmindedly picked up her old toy. 'Spider, Rose!' I said, and immediately her eyes opened, her ears pricked and she made an attempt at her juddering, bird-catching cry. I gave her the spider and she settled into a normal sleep. When she awoke she ate a small meal, and from that day gradually recovered her health and spirit.

The hunter

Nothing in the wild rivals the cat for the deadly accuracy and speed of its hunting; and no other species appears to take such delight in tormenting its prey. These ancestral instincts clearly emerge in the daily activities of the domestic cat. Play teaches the cat to think fast and to develop quick reactions which, in turn, train him to be a skilful hunter. Unfortunately, the victims are often beautiful garden birds, and it is virtually impossible to convey to your pet cat that although you approve of him keeping the rat and mouse population under control, you do not appreciate being presented with a mangled mass of feathers while you are busy grilling the breakfast bacon.

A bird, however, represents a real challenge to the cat's ingenuity. After the first few failures have at last

convinced him that the prey can fly up and away, he will develop a special technique for the final pounce. After the long, careful stalk, he will so judge his run and culminating leap as to compensate for the bird's take-off and trajectory. Lucifer, our large Foreign Red cat, had worked out this technique so accurately that he could sit on the outhouse roof and take the starlings in mid-air as they left their nests in the eaves.

It is not only the svelte Shorthairs that are so agile and cunning in this respect. We had a Longhaired Tortoiseshell, Coppapoppett, whose mouth would water whenever she sighted moorhen chicks on our small lake. The birds wisely nested on the little island in the centre of the lake and the nestlings took to the water as soon as they were hatched. Poppett would judder and drool as soon as the first fluffy little coal-black chicks appeared. We had to confine her to a wired run for three or four weeks until the young birds learned the meaning of fear, fleeing for the safety of the water at the least sign of danger. Not in the least deterred, the cat would lie in ambush for the half-grown chicks as they wandered onto the lawn, soon realizing that, rather than fly off, they preferred to scuttle along on their lanky legs back to the water. One day, I watched her getting into position at an angle between a solitary, grazing bird and the water's edge. As the moorhen saw its danger and scampered off to safety, she ran, not directly at the bird, but along a carefully planned tangential path so that they met with an audible thud on the bank. Luckily I was able to rescue this particular bird, but of the seven chicks hatched, only one lived to maturity.

In order to warn birds of her approach, we hung a couple of bells around Poppett's neck. This worked very well for a fortnight or so, until we found a dead thrush on the doormat. Poppett dashed past us indoors, bells still intact but not jangling. The mystery was solved when the builders working in the yard told us that they had seen her systematically rolling her neck from side to side in their sand heap. Sure enough, she had so jammed both bells with damp sand that the strikers could not function!

Curiously, although Poppett was so fond of fresh bird meat, she never attempted to stalk or catch any of our fantail pigeons. On the contrary, she would sit in the middle of some twenty or so of the birds, crunching up their meal, and they would show not the slightest sign of being afraid of her.

The developing brain

Recent research into the cat's brain development has shown that slight stress during early kittenhood helps to develop more active brain cells at a critical period in life, and also that frequent handling from the age of six to twelve weeks can determine the temperament of the adult cat. Involved as I am in the forming of new varieties of cats, I have had experimental litters over the years and had often noticed that the 'unusual' kittens in the family would grow up to be more friendly and intelligent than their 'ordinary' litter-

Below
A Burmese 'talking' as he walks through the grass. He is probably complaining about the unco-operative behaviour of the local mice.

Right
A handsome Tortoiseshell defying anyone to disturb him.

mates. I had always wondered whether this was due to some kind of hybrid vigour; but in the light of the new evidence, I now realize that it was always the 'new' kittens that were carefully checked several times daily and given extra handling at the critical period. Genetically, they were no cleverer than their litter-mates, but the early stress of prolonged handling and the later additional handling had clearly developed their full brain potential.

Jackie was the seventh kitten in a Siamese litter. He was born almost hairless and half the size of his brothers and sisters. Weak and weedy, he could not fight his way to the nipple, and by rights he should have died. Instead, I hand-reared him, feeding him every two hours, day and night, from an eye-dropper with evaporated milk and glucose. He grew into the strangest kitten I ever saw—all tummy, eyes and voice—and he could not bear to be left alone. I took him everywhere with me in a pigskin shoulder-bag, almost zippered across, and occasionally he would push his sooty little nose out and announce that it was mealtime.

At thirteen weeks of age, the litter was sold and Jackie, half normal size and still virtually hairless, was even now spending most of his time in my bag. We eventually asked my mother, who lived in the country, surrounded by the paddocks of a vast stud farm of thoroughbred horses, to give him a home. Nobody thought that Jackie would thrive or even live for long, but he surprised us all. On his first birthday he weighed in at a lusty nine pounds, his coat silky and immaculate, his points a dense, glossy seal-brown, and his sapphire eyes sparkling with health. He came up the path to the door, swaying importantly from side to side, the muscles in his neck standing up with the strain of carrying a large hare straddled between his legs. From that day Jackie decided that his purpose in life was to be a mighty hunter.

After one Sunday lunch, we washed up and put out the scraps, including half a Yorkshire pudding, into the pig-pail. About half an hour later we saw Jackie dragging the Yorkshire pudding onto the lawn, placing it carefully on the ground by a circular rose-bed. We watched incredulously as he settled down behind the screen of roses and waited until the starlings came down to the bait, when he began picking them off one by one.

Jackie's favourite pastime was to go on country walks with us, but he hated wet grass. So while we walked the rides between the oak-fenced paddocks of the stud farm, Jackie kept pace, treading sedately along the top rails, growling with annoyance each time he had to jump down to cross a ride or traverse some rough ground or grass.

The language of cats

Of all animals, the domestic cat surely least deserves the designation 'dumb'. Not only does it use its voice most expressively to communicate with other cats and with human companions, but it also employs a complex system of facial attitudes and bodily postures to convey very clearly and unmistakably its every wish and intention.

It expresses fright in several ways—its pupils dilate, its eyes flick rapidly from side to side, its coat and tail fluff up, and it turns its body, similarly ruffled, sideways so as to appear as big as possible, hoping thus to conceal fear. Warnings to would-be intruders are conveyed by the lashing of a tautly held tail, a withdrawal of the ears, a narrowing of the eyes and perhaps a menacing growl or two. The cat shows indifference by holding the tail straight up but in a relaxed state, usually following this by turning deliberately back and possibly undertaking a perfunctory grooming session. Extreme agitation is indicated by the tail in a rigid horizontal position, ears flat to the head and back slightly arched. This may be accompanied by muttered growls and much licking of lips and salivation.

The voice of the cat can be very expressive indeed. Each has its own unique range of mews, purrs and growls which an observant owner will soon recognize. There are the standard everyday demands to be let out, to come in and to be fed; and there are other noises to announce the approach of a stranger, to warn of impending danger or perhaps to herald a storm. The sight of a bird flying overhead or even glimpsed through a window elicits a special sound. An excited miaow punctuates play; and the mother cat reserves an entire range of special talk for her kittens. The kittens, in turn, each give out a different distress cry which may be heard and acted upon by the perceptive owner.

Cats, of course, have their own language of love, such as the caterwauling stimulation of a group of males squaring up to one another around a young female in oestrus, and the excited yip of the successful suitor as he makes his preliminary advances to his intended mate. Both male and female croon gently to each other when mating is imminent; a sharp purring call follows; and the growl of the mated female, loud and alarming, is quite unmistakable.

Perhaps the most endearing feature of the cat's character is its ability to relax utterly and completely, creating a calm, peaceful atmosphere, an aura of serenity around itself, even in the most disorderly, tempestuous household. How soothing it is, after a busy day, to sit quietly with a purring, sleepy cat upon one's knees, letting the same soporific feeling spread through one's whole being. How easy it is to understand why, when the little foraging cat first crept into the warmth of Stone Age man's fire, it was not eaten but welcomed as a companion. And no wonder this furry creature, with its immaculate habits and totally independent nature, went on to win a measure of human love and devotion unequalled by any other domesticated animal.

Index

abscesses 80
Abyssinian cat 6, 10, *50*, 53, 62, *63*, 67, *74*, *108*
'acting' cats 110, *111*, 112–13
Adastra 59
American Blue 67
American Shorthairs 23
American show procedure 90, 92
Angora cat 23
Archangel Blue 67

bandaging a cat 70
Beaumanor Becky 58
Bicoloured Longhair 30, *30*
Bicolour Shorthair 37
Big Kitten 100
Bimbo 113
Birman or Sacred cat 23, 31, *32*, 56
Black Persian 24, *25*, 30, *93*
Black Shorthair 32, 113
Black Smoke Persian *31*
Black and White Bicolour Shorthair 37
Black and White Persian 30
Blue Abyssinian 62
Blue Burmese 6, 7, 10, *57*, 58, 59, 62, *64*, *106*
Blue Chinchilla 31
Blue-Cream Burmese 59
Blue-Cream Cornish Rex *66*
Blue-Cream Persian 10, 28, *28*, 30
Blue-Cream Shorthair 35
Blue-eyed White Persian 24, *27*, 113
Blue-eyed White Shorthair 32, 35
Blue Persian 10, *22*, 24, 30, 32
Blue Point Persian 31
Blue Point Siamese 10, 53, *54*, 55, 62, *94*, *98*, 103, *103*, *106*
Blue Shorthair 32, 35, *79*
Blue Smoke Persian 28, *31*
Blue Spotted Shorthair 38
Blue Tortoiseshell Point Siamese *86*
Bonzo 59
brain development 124, 126
breeding 20–1, 55, 76, 85
Briarry Saccharin 60
Briarry Venus Improved 62
British Blue 10, *20*
British Shorthairs 23, 32–8, 119
British Tabby 36, 62
broken limbs 70
Bronze Egyptian Mau *60*
Brown Burmese 10, 56, *56*, 58, *102*, 103, *104*, *107*
Brown Spotted Shorthair 38
Brown Tabby Shorthair *35*, 36, *36*, *75*
Bryant, Doris 56
Burmese cat 10, 53, 56, 58–9, 103–7, *105*, *124*
Burmese Cat Club 59
Burmese Cat Society 58
Burmese/Siamese hybrid 53, 56, 59
buttering a cat's paws 49
buying a kitten 10, 13, 74

Calico Cat 37
Cameo Persian 31, 32, *33*
canker 13
Casa Gatos Darkee 58
Casa Gatos da Foong 58
cat as patient 69–70
Cat Fancy 58, 91, 92
cat-flap 14, *44*, 45

cat-nip mouse *86*
cat shows 85–93
catteries 46, *74*
Champagne Burmese 59
Champion Miskin 55
Chartreuse Blue *61*, *65*, 67
Chestnut Brown (Foreign) 60
'Child of the Gods' 62
Chinchilla 10, 24, 28, *29*, *39*, *89*, *110*, 112, 113, *113*
Chindwin's Minou Twm 58
Chinki Golden Gay 58
Chocolate Burmese 59
Chocolate Cream 59
Chocolate Point Persian 31
Chocolate Point Siamese 10, 53, 55, 60, *60*, *79*
Chocolate Tabby Point *60*
Clarissa 113
Clarke, Dora 60
claws 80, *80*
'coal-dust' specks 13
collars *74*
Colourpoints 10, 31, *72*, *84*
conjunctivitis 79, 80
Coppapoppett 124
Cora Capps 59
corneal ulcers 79
Cornish Rex *66*, 67, *67*, *90*
Craigiehilloch Bronze Leaf 60
Craigiehilloch Bronze Wing 60
Cream Burmese *57*, 59
Cream Cornish Rex *67*
Cream Persian 10, *23*, 24, 30, *109*
Cream Point Siamese 53
Cream Shorthair *34*, 35, *91*
Cream Spotted Shorthair 38
cross-eyes in Siamese 53
cystitis 82

Dandycat Brown Bear 60
Darshan Khudiran 58
deafness in white cats 24, 35, 62
Devon Rex 67
Diamonds are Forever 113
diarrhoea 82
Dido 59
diet *see* Feeding
diseases 75–6, 79–82
Doctor Doolittle 113
Dunnill, Mrs 60

ears 13, 17, 75, *75*, *81*
Egyptian Mau *60*, 62
El Maharanee Saengdao 62
Elizabethan collar 70, *70*
Elmtower Bronze Idol 60
Endless Night 113
European Shorthairs 23
eyes 13, 79, *79*

Fairlie Mehesso 62
Fairlie Menelic 62
Fatima 59
feeding 13, 17–18, 20, 41, 74
feline infectious anaemia 82
feline infectious enteritis 46, 75–6
feline infectious peritonitis 82
fish in diet 13, 18, 74
Fisher, Mrs 60

Flack, Elizabeth 61, 62
fleas 13, 16, 17, 45, 80
Florentine M'Bele 60
force-feeding 73
Foreign Black 62
Foreign Blue 62, 67
Foreign Lilac *60*, 61, 62
Foreign Red 124
Foreign Shorthairs 53–67, 122
Foreign Tabby 62
Foreign White *59*, 61, 62
Forestier-Walker, Miss 53
France, Lilian 58
French, Mrs 56, 59
Freeman, John 6
Frost Point Siamese *54*
furballs 16

Granny Grumps 56, 59
grooming 16, *18*, 24, 41, 45, *74*, 80, *80*

Hargreaves, Mrs 60
Harrison, Rex 113
Havana cat *58*, 59–60, *60*, 62
Himalayan Persian 30, 31
holidays, problems caused by 46
hunting instincts *43*, 122, 124

insecticides 74, 80
injuries, dealing with 49
internal disorders 81–2

Judd, Mrs 60

Kalaya Butterscotch 60
Kent, Mrs 59
kidney disease 82
kinks in Siamese cats' tails 53
Kipling, Rudyard 45
Kirby, Mrs 60
kitten pen *44*
kittening 21, 79
kittens:
    bed for kittens 13
    buying a kitten 10, 13, 74
    diseases 75–6
    feeding 13, 17–18
    introducing to the family 43
    kittens and children 43
    kittens and other pets 43–5
    moving kitten into its new home 42
    neutering and spaying 76
    patterns of behaviour 14–15
    playthings 15
    training to use litter tray 13
Korat cat *61*, 62
Korat Cat Fanciers' Association 62
Kye 113

language of cats 126
Lant, Miss 58
Laos Cheli Wat 58
Laurentide Arduo Prizm 60
Laurentide Aretoo Pearl 60
Lawrence, D. H. 98
lead, training to a *46*, 48, 49
lice 80
Lilac Egyptian Mau *60*

Lilac (Platinum) Burmese 59
Lilac Point Siamese 10, *45*, 53, *54*, 55, 61, 62, 113, 115
Lilac Point Persian 31
litter tray 13, 24, 49, 73
Longhairs 9, 10, 23–32, 91, 119; to groom 17, *80*
Lucifer 124
Lymphosarcoma 82

'Magpie' Longhair 30
Malay Self-Blue 62
Maltese Blue 67
Manx cat *9*, 10, 38, *38*
marmalade cat *19*
maternal devotion in cats 115–16
meat in diet 13
medicines, liquid, to give 73
military eczema 81
milk in diet 13, 18, 74
Mills, Hayley 113
minerals 18, 74
mites 80
Moggie 6
Monro-Smith 60
mouth 13, 79
moving house with a cat 48–9

National Cat Club Show, Olympia *88*, 89, 113
nephritis 82
neutering 16, 51, 76, 118
nose 13
nursing a cat 73–4

Odd-eyed White Persian 24
Odd-eyed White Shorthair 32, *35*, *78*
ointments, creams, to apply 73
Orange-eyed White Persian 24, *26*
Orange-eyed White Shorthair 32
Our Miss Smith 60

parasitic otitis 75
Pastel Siamese 55
Pastel Tabby Point Siamese 53
Persian cats 10, 23, 24. *See* Longhairs
photography of cats 109
playing, playthings 15, 43, 118, 122
pot-grown grass 24, *50*
pregnancy 76

quarantine regulations 46, 48

Red Abyssinian 62, *64*
Red Burmese 59
Red Persian 24, *27*, 28, 30
Red Point Persian 31
Red Point Siamese 10, 53, 55, *106*
Red Point Siamese-Rex *122, 123*

Red Spotted Shorthair 38
Red Tabby Persian 24
Red Tabby Shorthair *34*, 37
Red and White Bicolour Shorthair 37
Rex cat *66*, 67, *67, 123*
ringworm 80
roads, protecting cats from dangers of 49
Rochford, Marie 67
Rosie 122
roundworms 81
Royal Cat 53
Rumpy Manx 38
Russian Blue 60, *61*, 65, 67
Russian Blue Association 67
Russian cat 32

Sacred Cat 31, 56
Samsara Saburi 60
scent glands 116
Scintilla Copper Beech 60
Scott, Mr 60
scratching, scratching post 14, *15*, 24, 45, *45*
Seal Colourpoint 72
Seal Point Persian 31
Seal Point Siamese *19, 21*, 31, *52*, 53, 55, 56, 59, 60, 61, 62, *88, 96, 98, 99*, 113
Self Lilacs 61
Self Longhairs 24, 31
Sellers, Peter 112
Shaded Cameo Persian 32, *33*
Shaded Silver Persian 28
Shell Cameo Persian 32
Shorthairs 91, 124; British 10, 23, 32–8, 119; Foreign 53–67
showing cats 85–93
Siamese cat 10, *15*, 30, 32, 53, 55, 56, 58, 62, 91, 95–107, 113, 119, 122, 126. *See also* Blue Point etc
Siamese Cat Club 59
Siamese-Rex *123*
Siavana Feu Follette 60
Silver (Chinchilla) Point Siamese 55
Silver Spotted Shorthair *37*, 38, *44*
Silver Tabby 24, 36, *37, 44, 68, 75, 93, 110, 111*
skin disorders 80–1
Smoke Cameo Persian 32
Smoke Persian 28
Smoke Siamese 53, 55
Solitaire Maneki Neko 60
'Sorrel' cat *64*
Spanish Blue 67
Spanish cat 37
spaying 16, 51, 76
Spotted cats 36, 38
Stewart, Mrs 60
Stirling-Webb, Brian 61, 62
Stockley, Sister 59

strays, problem of 51
stomach 13
Stumpy Manx 38
Superstitions 113

tabby cats 32, 36, 38, *70*
Tabby Persians 24, *112*
Tabby Point Siamese 10, *15*, 53, 55, *55, 97*
tablets or pills, to give 73, *73*
tapeworms 81
tartar (or calculus) 79
teeth, care of 79
Thompson, Dr Joseph C. 56
Tib *112*
Timkey Browne 56, 59
tinned foods 13, 18
tom cats *16, 17*, 118
Tortie Burmese 59
Tortie Colourpoint *84*
Tortie Point Persian 31
Tortie Point Siamese 10, 53, 55, *55, 86*
Tortie Point Siamese-Rex *123*
Tortoiseshell 28, 30, *117*, 124, *125*
Tortoiseshell Burmese 59
Tortoiseshell Shorthair 37
Tortoiseshell and White Persian 28, *28*, 30
Tortoiseshell and White Shorthair *36*, 37
training cats for 'acting' work 110, 112–13
travelling with a cat 48
Tuptin 113
Turkish or Van cat 23, *30*, 31
Turner, Patricia 61, 62

Ullman, Miss Von 59
urolithiasis 82

Van cat *30*, 31
veterinary treatment 69–70, 74
viral respiratory infections 82
vitamins 18, 74
voice of a cat 126
vomiting 82
Vyvyan, Lady 53

Wander 59
Warren, Mrs 60
Weir, Harrison 53
Wendie 59
White Persians 10, 24, 32
White Shorthairs 32, 35
Winkie 59
Woodiwiss, Major 59
'working' cats 109–13, *110, 111*
Wrong Box, The 112

Young, Mrs Herbert 59

Acknowledgments

The publishers would like to thank the following organizations and individuals for their kind permission to reproduce the pictures in this book:

AFA Colour Library (G. Kinns): 118–119 above; Animal Graphics: 19 below, 27 above left, 38, 86–87, 109; Ardea (Su Gooders): 100; Barnaby's Picture Library: 27 above right, 70 below, 98, 199 below and contents; Sdeuard C. Bisserot: 26, 28 above, 61 left; Bruce Coleman Ltd (J. Burton): 21 (A. J. Deane): 121 below; W. S. Crawfords Ltd (Kosset Carpets): 110 right; Anne Cumbers: 15 below, 18 above, 28 below, 30, 34, 44 below, 45, 50, 52, 57 above, 67, 72, 74 left, 84, 88, 90 above, 91, 92–93 above, 110 left, 111 below right, 113; Daily Telegraph Colour Library: 54 above, 81; Robert Estall: 116; Fournier Rapho: 10; R. D. Hallmann: 29, 112, title and half-title; Louise Hughes: 77; Jacana Agence de Presse 12, 39, 42 below, 43, 48–49, 54 below, 65, 69, 74 right, 79 above, 122; Keystone Press Agency: 8; John Moss: 11; NHPA (S. Dalton): 16 (M. Davies): 111 above; Octopus Books: 68, 70 above, 70 centre, 73 left, 73 right, 75 above, 80; Pictor: 27 below, 71, 78, 83; Pictorial Press: 23, 55 below, 60; Spectrum Colour Library: 14, 17, 18 below, 19 above, 36, 40, 41, 44 above, 46, 56, 79 below, 99, 111 below left, 114, 117 above, 120, 125; The Sunday Times: 89, 101 below; Syndication International: 121 above; Sally Anne Thompson: 7, 9, 15 above, 20, 22, 25, 31, 32, 33, 35, 37, 42 above, 47, 51, 55 above, 57 below, 58, 59, 61 right, 63, 64 above, 64 below, 66, 75 below, 76, 90 below, 92 below, 94, 96, 97, 101 above, 102, 103, 104, 105, 106, 107, 108, 117 below, 123, 124.

PDO 77/373 1:6